WHEN
RAINS
BECAME
FLOODS

A Book in the series

LATIN AMERICA IN TRANSLATION / EN TRADUCCIÓN / EM TRADUÇÃO

 Sponsored by the Duke–University of North Carolina
Program in Latin American Studies

WHEN
RAINS
BECAME
FLOODS

A CHILD SOLDIER'S STORY

Lurgio Gavilán Sánchez

with the collaboration of YERKO CASTRO NEIRA
Foreword by CARLOS IVÁN DEGREGORI
Introduction by ORIN STARN
Translated by MARGARET RANDALL

DUKE UNIVERSITY PRESS / DURHAM AND LONDON / 2015

© 2015 Duke University Press
All rights reserved
Printed in the United States of America on acid-free paper ∞
Designed by Heather Hensley
Typeset in Quadraat Pro by Tseng Information Systems, Inc.

Library of Congress Cataloging-in-Publication Data
Gavilán Sánchez, Lurgio.
[Memorias de un soldado desconocido. English]
When rains became floods : a child soldier's story / Lurgio Gavilán
Sánchez ; with the collaboration of Yerko Castro Neira ; foreword
by Carlos Iván Degregori ; introduction by Orin Starn ; translated
by Margaret Randall.
Includes bibliographical references and index.
ISBN 978-0-8223-5842-8 (hardcover : alk. paper)
ISBN 978-0-8223-5851-0 (pbk. : alk. paper)
1. Gavilán Sánchez, Lurgio. 2. Child soldiers—Peru—Biography.
3. Sendero Luminoso (Guerrilla group—Biography. 4. Quechua
Indians—Peru—Biography. 5. Political violence—Peru—History—
20th century. 6. Peru—Politics and government—1980– I. Castro
Neira, Yerko. II. Randall, Margaret, 1936– III. Starn, Orin.
IV. Degregori, Carlos Iván. V. Title. VI. Series: Latin America
in translation/en traducción/em tradução.
F3448.7.G39a313 2015
985.06′4092—dc23
[B]
2014040372

Cover art: Author in uniform on the Huanta base, 1986.
Photographer unknown.

Original title in Spanish: *Memorias de un soldado desconocido. Autobiografía y antropología de la violencia* © 2012 Universidad Iberoamericana Ciudad de México.

For my children, Erick and Estela.
Don't let a day end
without having been happy,
without having fulfilled your dreams.

/ / /

And with sincere and profound gratitude
to Yerko Castro Neira
for helping this project find its way
into the world.

CONTENTS

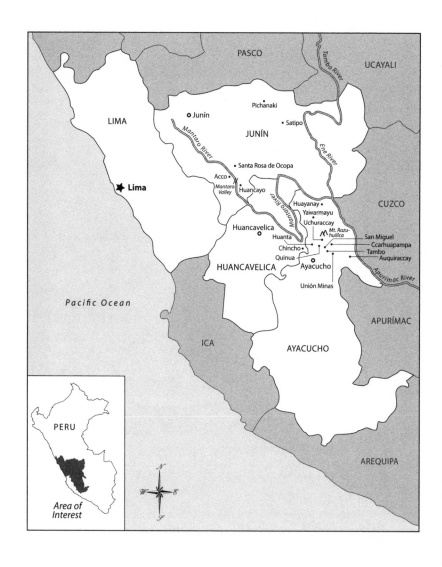

Map of the Ayacucho, Huancavelica, Junín, and Lima regions of Peru.

Carlos Iván Degregori

FOREWORD

Surviving the Flood: The Multiple Lives of Lurgio Gavilán

THIS IS AN EXCEPTIONAL BOOK. MORE PRECISELY, THIS IS THE HIS-
tory of an exceptional life. Lurgio Gavilán was a child soldier in the
ranks of the Shining Path guerrillas. He was not recruited, nor was
he kidnapped or taken by force, a common practice in the years following those in which Gavilán joined the organization. At the age
of twelve, he decided to join to follow in his brother's footsteps. He
wanted to see the world, to change the world—at least his world—
which was on the margins of, though not marginal to, the rest of the
country.

It was the beginning of 1983. Shining Path, as he put it, "flooded
the countryside," and for many of the rural poor, its totalitarian nature wasn't yet apparent. And so its authoritarian rigidity was accepted in many places as an expression of the "toughness" necessary
for restoring an order that seemed unjust or nonexistent. The army
had just arrived in Ayacucho.

With his Little Red Book, which he couldn't read, under his arm,
the boy Lurgio, a guerrilla fighter now, wandered over peaks and
through valleys (more over peaks, to tell the truth, including Apu Razuhuillca, the highest mountain in the northern part of Ayacucho).[1]
He saw the burning of villages, witnessed more than a few deaths,
participated in combat, and took part in executions of adolescents
like himself whom Shining Path condemned for errors such as falling asleep on nightly guard duty or, like the young girl who cooked for
and deloused the troops, "because, they said, she had fallen in love

with a policeman in Tambo." Some young people began to become aware that they were part of the horror and terror: "Little by little we began to understand that the Party was a monster that assassinated its own people." They talked among themselves about the possibility of escape, but how and where? By this time they were hated by many of the peasants, whose violence could be equally cruel. "Of course, how could they not have hated us if we had burned their village?" Gavilán remembers.

Two years after joining Shining Path, Gavilán is wounded in battle. An army officer who approaches with the intention of putting a bullet in his head sees a dirty adolescent boy who looks even younger after two years of living from hand to mouth. He drags him to his feet, ready to shoot. Gavilán feels fear but acts brave; he has to die "shouting long live Shining Path!"

At the last minute the officer feels pity for Gavilán and decides to take him with them. During the entire journey, the village patrollers (*ronderos*) implore the officer to kill the terrorist (*terruco*). Gavilán, who speaks almost no Spanish, is protected by the officer and ends up at Los Cabitos camp, in La Mar province (which happened to share the name of the main regional army base), the notorious location of the crematoriums, where those who entered lost all hope.[2]

At Los Cabitos the officer burns Gavilán's lice-covered clothes. Gavilán discovers that he isn't the only refugee, that there are several girls and boys, former terrorists like him, also living in the barracks. His gratitude survives today, although he also knew of "Shining Path prisoners who served the soldiers' sexual appetites and were later assassinated."

As a child soldier in the Peruvian army, Gavilán ends up going to school in Huanta. He is a model student, earning the confidence of the young officers, and adapting to military life. When he turns eighteen, he reenlists in the army, rising eventually to become a sergeant, and then his life takes another dramatic turn. I will leave the details for him to relate, but Gavilán later abandons the army to become a novice with the Franciscans at the colonial convent of the Alameda de los Descalzos in Lima.

And, then, in yet another turn, Gavilán leaves the army to study anthropology at San Cristóbal University in Huamanga province, an institute of higher learning itself healing from the terrifying war years.[3] Once again, he is an outstanding student. Soon he is named assistant professor, and a few years later he earns one of the scholarships offered by the Ford Foundation through the Institute of Peruvian Studies. Currently he is at the Ibero-American University in Mexico City, the institution that originally published this extraordinary autobiography.

I got to know Gavilán at the Institute of Peruvian Studies. He is contained and soft-spoken, with a gentle personality. "How did you ever get to be a sergeant with that voice?" I ask him. "I can yell too," he says. It was at the convent, in the waning evening hours when he would be reading the day's epistle or a passage from the Bible, that they taught him he didn't necessarily have to speak in that military tone or feel obliged to shout. Today he is sparing even in his gestures; only once did I see tears in his eyes, and that was when we said goodbye: he was leaving for Mexico, and I was ill.

His itinerary resembles him. This memoir is centered in those provinces that have been most battered by violence in all Peru—La Mar, Huanta, and Huamanga—but it doesn't overwhelm the reader with bloody details. He tells everything, or almost everything, but without getting lost in the most brutal stories. Although Quechua is his first language, his Andean Spanish is nevertheless extremely beautiful, and he employs turns of phrase and regional cadences in that language that enrich the text.

A contribution of this book is that it helps to humanize the members of Shining Path, especially those in its lower ranks, and moves past the simplistic idea that they were a kind of "incarnation of evil."[4] Hundreds of child soldiers and thousands of adolescents or very young adults were drawn to the organization by its discourse and some of its actions. They weren't aliens from another planet. Sufficient time has passed for us to try to understand in greater detail who these people were, why they did what they did, how a totalitarian ideology took them in—at least for a time—and how the terrorist project came to describe a veritable parable.[5] Hundreds are now reintegrated into society, many without even having served prison time. The vast majority of these people are totally immersed in new lives. Some may feel a degree of nostalgia for bygone times, or continue to espouse radical ideas or lifestyles, but they no longer favor political violence. Only a very few continue on that path.[6]

This reality and this autobiography both say a great deal about that which, in another article, I have called Shining Path pyramid.[7] Gavilán was at the base of that pyramid. He didn't become a village patroller, like so many others, but a soldier instead. He didn't really have an alternative. And when he returned to his village he found it destroyed: without a school, without a future. Everything had to be (re)built.

There are few autobiographies by child soldiers. We have one by Ishmael Beah—now a young adult of Sierra Leone, joyous, talkative, sporting dreads, wearing a three-piece suit and "brilliant brow," as his family described him as a child—and happy to be in New York when I met him.[8] His story is radically different, just as the conflict in Sierra Leone was different, but it does have some points of similarity with Gavilán's.

There are more biographies of perpetrators but, as Leigh Payne has called them, these are "unsettling accounts," in which neither repentance nor reconciliation appear.[9] In Lurgio Gavilán's book, especially in the last chapter, "Twenty Years Later," when he returns to the places he inhabited as a child soldier, it is clear that violence belongs to the past. The very experience of writing this book, most of which he did in the Franciscan convent, has been an exercise in leaving the past behind, and in reconciling with himself. "I don't hold bitterness toward anyone. Little by little I matured. Life has just begun."

Orin Starn

INTRODUCTION

WE SOMETIMES RECEIVE STRANGE OMENS OF WHAT LIES AHEAD.
One gray dawn, almost forty years ago now, a dead dog was found
hung from a lamppost in downtown Lima. No one seemed to know
just who would have done such a thing, or why. Clearly, however,
those responsible wanted to send a message to the new Chinese prime
minister, Deng Xiaoping. They had picked a lamppost not far from the
Chinese embassy and left a crude sign around the dog's neck. "Deng,"
it read, "you son of a bitch." The police cut down the unfortunate animal, a few newspapers ran stories, and Peru's sprawling, grimy capital went about its business.

The macabre canine mystery foretold a long and bloody war. It was
1980, and the American hostages were still captive in Iran, Margaret
Thatcher and Ronald Reagan were rising to power, and John Lennon
was soon to be murdered outside his Manhattan apartment building. The dog had been strung up by militants of a then largely ob-
scure Maoist faction called Sendero Luminoso, or Shining Path (and
it was later learned they had left others with similar placards elsewhere around the country).[1] These hard-line revolutionaries detested

Publisher's note: The original Spanish-language edition of this book included an
introduction by the Chilean anthropologist Yerko Castro Neira. (See note 21
below for more on his role in bringing *When Rains Became Floods* to publication.)
A translation of Castro Neira's introduction, provided by the Universidad
Iberoamericana, is available on the Duke University Press website at www
.dukepress.edu/When-Rains-Became-Floods/.

Deng for steering China away from command socialism and toward the market economy. The dead dogs were an early propaganda salvo in their fight to establish a Peruvian People's Republic modeled on Mao's Cultural Revolution and its missionary Marxist zealotry. Shining Path militants believed that the Soviet Union and Cuba had also strayed too far from the true socialist pathway. They wanted to take charge themselves of raising the revolutionary torch toward the new century.[2]

Leading Shining Path was Abimael Guzmán, a former philosophy professor at Huamanga University in the Andean city of Ayacucho. He founded the Peruvian Communist Party, as the rebels called themselves, in the late 1960s, and in 1980 ordered their first armed attacks.[3] A cult of personality arose around Guzmán, Chairman Gonzalo to his followers, and party propaganda anointed him as "the Fourth Sword of Marxism" in a royal Communist Party lineage from Marx to Lenin to Mao. What the revolutionaries termed "Marxism-Leninism-Maoism, Gonzalo Thought" became their guiding ideology. They planned first to seize power in Peru and then bring down capitalism worldwide. Victory, Guzmán promised, was certain. "We will demolish imperialist domination and the reactionaries" he declared, "and we will wipe them off the face of the earth."[4]

It was madness, of course: the pseudoscientific Marxist jargon, the bogus Dear Leader cult, the absurd expectations. What chance had a few backwater rebels of taking over the planet? Only a few thousand Peruvians ever did join Shining Path. But the group's fervor made it what the influential Peruvian intellectual Carlos Iván Degregori termed a "dwarf star," namely a burning force out of proportion to its modest size.[5] Shining Path gained control over parts of Peru's impoverished southern highlands in the early 1980s, and the country's president sent in the military. Their brutal battle, with local villagers massacred by both sides, plunged the region into chaqwa, the Quechua word for suffering and chaos. The guerrillas also expanded their Lima operations. There they killed policemen and politicians and, as a scare tactic, blew up electrical towers to pitch the capital into darkness (even though, as I recall from living in Lima then, thousands of gas-powered generators would soon afterward roar to life across the pragmatic city). Abimael Guzmán, the small-town philosophy professor, became his country's most wanted man, the Osama Bin Laden of that time.

Everything came crashing down in the end. As the war dragged across the decade, many villagers grew disenchanted with Shining Path; they began forming *rondas*, or local militias, to drive the guerrillas from their former Andean strongholds.[6] And then in 1992 a police swat team captured Guzmán in his apartment hideout upstairs from a ballet studio in a wealthy Lima district.[7] So certain was the Shining Path helmsman about his own invincibility that he had not bothered to encode the party membership rosters discovered there. The information helped the police to round up almost the entire Shining Path leadership. They displayed Guzmán to the press corps in a *Silence of the Lamb*–style cage and then locked him away in a navy island prison off Lima's coast. Only a few guerrilla remnants remained at large, far out toward the jungle, the war effectively over.

But the damage had been done. The war had cost an already poor, divided country more than $1 billion in damages and had left more than a half million refugees and at least sixty-nine thousand people dead.[8] The memories of those who vanished in the violent storm still hang over the highlands now decades later. "Where could she be?" asks a ballad by the master Ayacuchan songwriter Ranulfo Fuentes; "Perhaps under the stony ground/becoming earth/or among the thorns/budding like wildflowers."[9]

/ / /

IT WAS IN THE HEADY EARLY DAYS that Lurgio Gavilán joined Shining Path. He was just twelve years old and the third of five children from a poor peasant family in the Ayacuchan countryside.[10] These windy highlands were a region of almost Fourth World poverty, with no running water, electricity, or other basic services. Villagers made their homes in straw and mud farmhouses scattered amid the gigantic green Andean peaks. Gavilán spent his first years in the hamlet of Auquiraccay. Many families there also had land in the jungles that lay a day or two's walk down the steep foggy footpaths to the east. Gavilán's parents eventually settled by the Apurímac River's tropical banks. They could only afford to send Gavilán to school for a few years, and he did not learn to read or write. The boy spoke only the local indigenous Quechua tongue.

Shining Path was rising in the region. Their Maoist blueprint dictated first controlling the countryside so as then, as Guzmán put it with his accustomed vehemence, to "strangle" the cities. The promise of a new, just order found traction among a peasantry who had suffered discrimination, hunger, and marginalization for so long. Gavilán's older brother had joined a roving guerrilla column; Gavilán followed out of family loyalty and idealism and with few other possibilities for a poor Andean boy. The party expected its militants to give the so-called quota, namely, to die and to kill for the greater revolutionary good. Those who tried to desert were stoned, hung, or shot in front of the others. Gavilán's little band lived a frozen, half-starved life on the run, hunted by green army helicopters and village militiamen, as often as not tortured to death when captured. Gavilán fought with Shining Path for a little over two years. Finally, still only fifteen, he was taken prisoner by an army patrol that had starved his column out of rocky Razuhuillca Mountain.

This extraordinary memoir, so beautifully translated by Margaret Randall, describes Gavilán's guerrilla years. As our only insider account about life in Shining Path, When Rains Became Floods is a first. It also happens to be a magical, devastating, powerful piece of writing (and no less a literary star than the Peruvian Nobel laureate Mario Vargas Llosa admiringly hailed its original Spanish publication).[11] Like every really good book, this one takes unexpected turns, sharp here. Gavilán, his life spared, became a soldier himself, fighting now against his former guerrilla comrades, and then later a Franciscan priest. Each of the three clannish organizations to which he belonged—Shining Path, the army, and the church—proved to be a strange and sometimes terrifying enchanted island in its own way. When Rains Became Floods is a latter-day Andean Odyssey, with Gavilán, like his ancient Ithacan prototype, also somehow managing to survive the hardships, temptations, and perils of a long journey in search of his own place in the world.

It is with Shining Path that Gavilán begins his story. We already have many other Latin American guerrilla war memoirs. One thinks, for example, of Ernesto "Che" Guevara's Diary, about the iconic Argentine rebel's failed fight to overthrow Bolivia's then military dictatorship.[12] Gavilán also recounts almost unimaginable sacrifice, suffering, and struggle powered by dreams for a more just society. Yet *When Rains Became Floods* is no paean to the revolutionary road. To the contrary, Gavilán describes the deadly contradictions at Shining Path's crimson heart. The guerrillas promised democracy and equality in the new revolutionary order. Their own internal organization, however, mirrored the oppressive Peruvian hierarchy of color and class dating back to the Spanish conquest five centuries before. Here Guzmán and his mostly white, city-dwelling inner circle commanded a young, poor, brown-skinned army from village stock. Shining Path, good Maoists, claimed the peasantry would be the revolution's backbone, and yet they slaughtered villagers by the thousands for siding with the army or just seeking to remain neutral. I recall the weeklong journey I made on foot through the Ayacuchan highlands toward the war's end. As much as I had heard about atrocities, it was shocking to walk through one brutalized hamlet after another and to listen to the survivors' tales about Shining Path torching houses, kidnapping children to become fighters, and hacking villagers to death in predawn attacks. Guzmán's troops bore responsibility for some two-thirds of the war dead.[13]

It was tempting, back then, to regard Shining Path as an anomaly. Like Cambodia's Khmer Rouge, their fight seemed a case of Marxism devolving into mass murder. The reality, as we look back now across the decades, is that extreme brutality in the revolutionary Communist cause was not uncommon: Lenin's pogroms, Stalin's gulags, Mao's purges. (And, it should be underscored, what we have learned about supposedly liberty-loving America's own secret assassinations, torture manuals, and backing for bloody dictatorships is hardly cause for pride either.) It was Marxism's magnetic promise to do away with capitalism's savage inequalities to build an egalitarian earthly paradise. So noble was the goal that even the bloodiest means could seem justified in achieving it. "You have to break eggs," as Stalin supposedly put it, "to make an omelet." Gavilán grew disgusted with Shining Path's especially unapologetic, almost ecstatic intention to "crush," "annihilate," and "pulverize" those in its way. This book, then, stands less in the tradition of Che than of a Václav Havel or Andrei Sakharov. It bears witness to how far Marxism could go wrong and, in Peru and too many other places, lead to so much blood, death, and sacrifice for nothing.

That Gavilán was so young gives his account a particular poignancy. We know from books, films, and sometimes their own memoirs about African children dragged into wars like those in the Congo, Sudan, and Sierra Leone. In the longer view, of course, there have always been child soldiers—the boy David slaying Goliath; Napoleon's drummer boys; Warsaw ghetto resistance fighters; and, for that matter, American teen gang members in drug battle zones. In Peru, too, anthropologist Jessaca Leinaweaver notes the phenomenon of "child circulation," namely how poor Andean children may be sent to live and sometimes work with relatives in other places.[14] These flexible kin relations have served, among other things, as a strategy for navigating precarious economic circumstances that make the stable nuclear family a luxury many Peruvians cannot afford. At twelve, Gavilán had already left his parent's jungle homestead, and in fact he was in the highlands planting potatoes with relatives when he followed his brother into Shining Path. He found many other kids his age among the guerrillas, an army of lost boys and girls.

Yet Shining Path was another world. Some children, like Gavilán, joined more or less on their own; others were taken away at gunpoint from mountain homesteads to be made into fighters. For young recruits, the column became family, a ragtag little band with no way back home. One teenage fighter was strangled to death, Lord of the Flies style, for stealing some crackers and tuna, a warning against disobedience of any kind. "Forgiveness," Gavilán explains, "did not exist in the party." If Gavilán and many others lost faith in the fight eventually, the ties between them remained strong through it all. Gavilán describes his special bond with Rosaura, a high-spirited Andean beauty of nineteen who became his surrogate big sister. (And Shining Path, much more than most other Latin American guerrilla movements, recruited many women into its ranks.)[15] Gavilán and Rosaura would join the others to sing revolutionary anthems at their nighttime camps ("Down with imperialism! Down! Long live our freedom!"). "The songs," Gavilán recalls, "made us feel as if we were made of steel, but we were human, children, peasants shouting among the lifeless rocks with no one listening." Gavilán was fleeing an army ambush with Rosaura when a bullet shattered her arm, and then another left her bleeding to death on the mountain.

Gavilán would be captured the next day. He was grateful to the lieutenant who spared his life, and, as a homeless fifteen-year-old, he decided that staying in the army was his best and perhaps only option. Such side-switching was quite common by that time. The guerrillas had promised a better world. A decade later, their war had only brought misery and suffering, and villagers could see that Chairman Gonzalo would not, as Gavilán had once believed, "appear at any moment in a helicopter and do away with the soldiers." Sympathy for Shining Path never ran very deep. The Peruvian military, too, scaled back its more indiscriminate brutality for a more savvy mix of threats, handouts, and promises to win over the peasantry. Some villages turned against the guerrillas almost overnight, much as Gavilán did. *Rondas*, the local anti–Shining Path militias, gained rapid strength across the Andes, bolstering the counterinsurgency. If the Andes had witnessed powerful rebellions going back to the eighteenth-century neo-Incan Túpac Amaru and before, this latest one, paradoxically enough, was partly brought down by the very peasant masses Shining Path's Maoist blueprint had predicted would be the most diehard revolutionaries.[16] Guzmán's capture, the corrupt Lima establishment rushing to crow over his downfall, only hastened the end of a war already being lost in the mountains.

Gavilán remained in the army for seven years. He began, still too young to enlist formally, as an errand boy; then he was a lowly private, finally rising to sergeant. By contrast to the archetypal right-wing Latin American militaries of, say, Chile and Argentina, the Peruvian army had a populist tradition; its so-called military socialist junta of the late 1960s carried out a major land reform intended to benefit the rural poor. The army was also among the few avenues of social mobility for penniless, brown-skinned young men in a Peru whose hierarchy of color and class led some to compare it to South Africa under apartheid. Yet barracks life was hard. There were nighttime patrols in the icy mountains and capricious commanders with pseudonyms like Centurion, Lieutenant Shogun, and the Big Banana, not to mention the danger still of Shining Path attacks. Here, too, Gavilán witnessed firsthand the military's brutality, including secretly executing captured guerrillas. Gavilán and the other troops, while marching in town, would sing: "Terrorist/if I find you/I will eat your head" (and only later, as the military tried to win people over, changed to "Good day, the soldiers of Peru salute you").

A chance encounter led to yet another abrupt life change. Nuns from the Congregación Jesús Verbo y Víctima (Jesus Verb and Victim Congregation) now and then traveled with Gavilán's unit for protection. One, as she got to know the young sergeant, suggested that he consider the priesthood. The Catholic Church in Peru was, as elsewhere in Latin America, deeply divided. Advocates for what the pioneering Peruvian Dominican Gustavo Gutiérrez famously termed "liberation theology" believed the Church should prioritize the fight for social justice and the poor. They clashed with conservatives like the Lima archbishop Juan Luis Cipriani, an outspoken opponent of homosexuality, human rights activists, and other "unholy" forces. By then Gavilán was no longer the illiterate little Indian boy who had joined Shining Path, and yet he knew and cared little about larger debates within the Church. He became a priest in order to leave war behind, serve the needy, and atone for what he felt to be his own wartime sins. As a wandering Franciscan, he become "homeless once again . . . like the lilies and the birds in the countryside," except now under Christ's white flag and not the red hammer and sickle.

It is an amazing story, and yet what makes *When Rains Became Floods* so special is Gavilán's telling of it. The book resembles a long Andean Zen prose poem in its spare yet haunting way. Gavilán wastes no words, and in this sense he writes in the tradition of the sad *huayno* ballads still so popular across the Andes. These compact songs frequently draw imagery from the natural world—the yellow flower in the rocks, the little bird's delicate song—to evoke the pain of lost love, homesickness, and poverty. For his part, Gavilán pauses at various moments to recall an evening's thin pink light, a mountain morning's stillness, or talking to an eagle who perched near the military base. These little parentheses do not always serve any larger allegorical purpose. Gavilán wants to account for the rocks, the trees, the animals, and the rain because they also belong to this world of ours where life itself can sometimes take flight as fast as a mountain lark winging into the grey-blue sky.

It might be possible to see some primordial indigenous worldview at work. But this would, I think, be a disservice to Gavilán. His view of the interconnectedness of humans, animals, and the land is indeed rooted in an Andean way of understanding quite different from a more conventional Western outlook. But the Andes have never been the pristine Shangri-La of the tourist postcards and travel brochures, despite the region's outsized, almost mythical history and geography. Villagers nowadays migrate between the countryside, Lima, and sometimes Europe and the United States; join evangelical churches; check in with relatives on their cell phones; and otherwise belong fully to our shrinking modern world. Gavilán's own journey exposed him to varied influences that left their mark. He recalls for us, music threaded into his tale, the lyrics to Maoist anthems, barracks chants, and Franciscan vespers. *When Rains Became Floods* bears traces, among other things, of Gavilán's religious training and the archetypal biblical themes of sin, suffering, and rebirth, if never exactly redemption. He lists Franz Kafka and José Saramago among his literary inspirations.[17] This, then, is a son of the Andes, and yet no "typical" anything. *When Rains Became Floods* is all Gavilán's own, and a sometimes brilliant literary creation at once all too real, dream-like, and different from any other book I know.

If a single theme runs through the tale, it is the almost magical capacity of certain institutions and ideologies to shape lives. Gavilán marched under three banners—the Communist hammer-and-sickle, the Christian white, and, as a soldier, the Peruvian national flag. All three had a vertical command structure that demanded absolute obedience from their followers. Each proffered its own sacred articles of faith, whether Chairman Gonzalo's teachings, the glories of Peruvian patriotism, or the Word of God. A horrifying hypermachismo pervaded military culture. Soldiers in Gavilán's barracks brutalized prostitutes and raped captured prisoners. By contrast, the Franciscans demanded chastity, and Shining Path discouraged and sometimes punished love in war. Gavilán, while clear about these and other differences, shows how dangerous it can be to subsume one's own will to any greater crusade. Yet this book is not some simple morality play about the hazards of groupthink. Gavilán also conveys the attractions and sometimes joys of comradeship, purpose, and belonging for a meaning-seeking and social species like ours, no matter what that larger cause may be. He manages throughout his tale to combine strong, sometimes heart-wrenching feeling with a seer's meditative distance from petty worldly judgment.

As he turns in his Franciscan habit to pursue a university degree, Gavilán is left with his memories. The war's end led to various attempts to reckon with its human costs, among them street art, a memory museum, and a Truth and Reconciliation Commission appointed by the national government.[18] In reality, of course, we can never make the past right, or even agree on what lessons should be learned from it. The war divided many Andean hamlets, turning neighbors into what anthropologist Kimberly Theidon has termed "intimate enemies."[19] Some villagers, uninterested in opening old wounds, refused to speak to Truth and Reconciliation Commission investigators, or wanted money to do so.[20]

The commission itself, once more mirroring archetypal Peruvian hierarchies, was mostly made up of white Lima-based intellectuals and activists, with not a single Quechua speaker among them. Top military officials wanted to shut down any investigation of their war crimes. Shining Path leaders, also anything but repentant, still issued occasional pronouncements about world revolution's inevitability from their jail cells. Many Peruvians have little interest in recalling a war that ended before the younger generation was even born. Their everyday concerns, like so many of us nowadays, revolve more around making a living, the latest on Facebook, Twitter, and Instagram, friends, family, and dreams for the future.

Gavilán gives us this book in the hope, however tenuous, that greater understanding may help ensure that nothing like the war "will ever happen in Peru again."[21] As much as anything, *When Rains Became Floods* nonetheless reads as a personal reckoning, as the account of a man, in his words, "standing before life's mirror." Gavilán wants to make some sense of his past, and as he puts it, "memories are like a journey through endless time." But he has no truck with platitudes about trauma, healing, or any point of final resolution. "I felt," he writes at one point, "as if memory was feeding in my blood, like fleas or white lice did when I lived clandestinely and walked with my rifle in my hand, reading the bible of Mao Tse-tung." Remembering brings Gavilán both pain and pleasure; much about the past remains a mystery to him, as it must be to us all.

As much as he has seen, Gavilán is still quite young, barely forty at this writing. The little boy from Auquiraccay has already lived three very different lives, and now, as an anthropologist, has embarked on a fourth. It was reading the influential mid-twentieth-century Peruvian writer and anthropologist José María Arguedas that first drew Gavilán to the field, and he counts now Frantz Fanon, Michel Foucault, and Edward Said among his other influences. Anthropology, he explains, has furnished him a way to better understand the costs of war and suffering, and the changing realities in his native Ayacucho.[22] This new career and his two young children have once again given Gavilán what he describes as "reasons to go on living."

We are very fortunate to have his extraordinary book.

La Mar province, Ayacucho, where we fought in 1983 and 1984.
Photograph by author, 2002.

IN THE RANKS OF SHINING PATH 1

I write this history in order to retrieve my memory; and also so nothing like it will happen again in Peru.

Verba volant, scripta manent (Words fly away, what is written remains). In the spirit of this Latin phrase, and encouraged by a professor at the School of Pontifical and Civil Theology in Lima, today I decide to tell my story from the age of twelve, when I followed my brother into the ranks of Shining Path (*Sendero Luminoso*). She said: "Why don't you write about your life?" I often hesitated, asking myself: Who would be interested in a story like mine? Would writing it enable Peru to know a guerrilla fighter? Would it allow Peru to understand something of human suffering? Would it keep history from repeating itself? What could it possibly be good for? Now I simply prefer—as José Carlos Mariátegui said—that the work speak for itself.[1]

This is how I got the courage to talk about what I have lived. I hope my story contributes to human understanding, and that others may share the sentiments of this writer and of those I portray here, because our lives are like soap bubbles: from the moment they exist they begin to die. As we make our way through life, in that long process of dying we shoulder and then discard our cultural baggage.

This autobiography was written between 1996 and 1998 and finished in 2000.[2] I filled in the empty spaces in 2007 and 2010. This was how I was able to complete the book and put a few of my memories into words. This is not a history of violence, but rather a series of stories about ordinary life, devoid of theatrics and party politics.

In no way do I try to justify the atrocities committed by Shining Path or the Peruvian army; I simply tell the events as they occurred. For this writer, these are ordinary memories, as if I lived them only yesterday. An unknown soldier's life takes many twists and turns. They are not all here, perhaps because some of the memories are distant now, or some are less important.

When we children had not yet reached adolescence we were already fighting in the so-called people's war. Back then, the idea was to contribute to the needs of a new nation, one that was more developed, with greater justice and equality, where man's exploitation of man did not exist. But it all disintegrated into humans acting worse than beasts to one another and into times of suffering (*waqay vida*).[3]

All this has to do with something I have always asked myself, always wanted to know: what is Peru? Is it made up of soulless Indians, as the first religious men who came to the New World believed, or simply a lot of beggars seated on golden benches, as Antonio Raymondi wrote?[4]

Peru is a multicultural and diverse nation with many bloods, an amalgam of cultures with a discriminatory idiosyncrasy. When have we ever been one Peru, a country united?

Sometimes I think we are united (*huklla*) only when our soccer players wear their "red and white" and get our people to joyously scream the word "goal"; or when we raise on high the red-and-white flag, or simply a red one, as if begging for help. What passions fire our blood? What notion do we have of the country in which we live? What temporal meaning do these symbols express? Will they endure? Or, as the *cumbia* sung by a northern musical group proclaims about love: "will they appear and disappear."[5]

Peru is a country as complicated as its idiosyncrasies, as the indignation of its people or its momentary, regional, family, or individual conflicts. So when does resentment, vengeance, and rebellion explode? When Peru becomes aware that it lives in a deceptive system? When the level of hunger is greater than the daily possibilities of subsistence? When, tired of democratic utopias and political parties, people say "enough" and rise up?

As we have seen, our leaders have invented constitutions in order to legitimize their power, hiding within the judicial apparatus a language that gets more perverse by the day.[6] Our political constitutions have not been documents of rights but models for structuring the state. We live in constant anxiety, trying this and that, always beginning again at zero and never getting anywhere. We have too much faith in the virtues of politicians, in presumed saviors, in the pretty phrases "the government is for all Peruvians," or the government with a "human face."[7]

I am left with the words of Saint Francis of Assisi: "Brothers, let us begin, we have done little or nothing," or with the universal poet César Vallejo's judgment: "sadly, humans . . . brothers there is much to be done."[8]

It is true that, as one remembers one experiences a kind of nostalgia, but at the same time there is a lightening of the spirit. I lived for many years in the ranks of Shining Path, in military barracks, in a Franciscan convent, in peasant communities, and in centers of academic learning.

MY FIRST EXPERIENCES IN THE RANKS OF SHINING PATH

It was the month of January 1983. My uncle and I were traveling from the rain forest to the mountains to visit my relatives in Auquiraccay.[9] We carried some foodstuffs from the region (potatoes, geese, broad beans). It's a two-day trip by foot. And so we journeyed, through mountains, forest, and deep gorges.

"Where will you be tomorrow," my father asked—a day before my departure for Auquiraccay—as he looked toward the solitary hills that appeared blue in the distance at the hour of dusk (pantaq), when the sky stretching west was tinted with orange, a premonition of nostalgia.

I left my community weeks after the massacre at Uchuraccay.[10] It was the rainy season, when peanuts are planted. It was the time when the first mangoes, oranges, and tangerines begin to ripen, and appear yellow as glints of light through the thick green forest of the Apurímac River.

Shining Path had also appeared at that time and in that place, imi-

The rain forest of the Apurímac River. Photograph by author.

tating the dark clouds of the south. Clouds don't always come filled with good rain. They often flood the fields or destroy the crops. That's how Shining Path came to my community, disguised as good rain. The first drops gave us hope for life, for social justice. But the rains lasted longer and longer. And fear appeared, because the water began to destroy and clean away "all that was old." And so we began to live the "flood."

There was nothing to do but to climb aboard Shining Path's ark or join the village militias (*rondas campesinas*).[11] Shining Path leader Chairman Gonzalo's words were coming true: "A blood bath is needed," because, according to him, there couldn't be an authentic revolution without spilling blood.[12] And "when the flood passes," in the new state, under socialism, we will plant uncontaminated crops once more.[13]

In 1983, that year of heavy rain, I went with my uncle to Auquiraccay, along a switchback path that runs serpentine from where the Ayacucho rain forest begins. It is the path used by the peasants of Punqui, Huarcca, Anyay, and Anco. They move with their beasts of burden, back and forth between the mountains and the forest. If it is time to

My uncle and aunt harvesting corn at the farm where I lived as a child. Photograph by author.

plant potatoes, it is necessary to travel to the mountains and come right back to the rain forest, to plant peanuts or harvest coca leaves. This is why I went to Auquiraccay: to plant potatoes, visit my relatives who lived there, and return with goods from the region.

The route from rain forest to mountains passes through country that is cold and country that is hot; the ecology changes from zone to zone. The lonely *ichus* sway in the cold mountain wind. The precious orchids and berries, those sweet and sour little fruits, grow along the way to provide food for the wild animals and for the peasants too.

Country people have traveled these places for a long time. Each year they weed and clear the pathways. Keeping them clear was always a fiesta. Each community was in charge of its area, and so they came together in a gathering (*tupay*). The song (*qarawi*) of the women encouraged the workers. The lieutenant, with his whip in hand, kept an eye on those who didn't work.[14] Fermented *chicha* nourished the workers and made them drunk. Fights were common. This was the way it was before, in the decade of the 1970s. Now it has changed.

When we were small, we would get tired walking and our father would mount us on horseback for the journey from rain forest to mountains. The trip took two days, sometimes three if the horses got tired of trotting. Seated comfortably, at ease with the rhythm of the horses' gentle gait, we would observe the native landscape. "Look at that bird over there," we would say. In those places nature immerses you in a wonderful world: "hanging" waterfalls with their transparent waters, cold and sweet. Our father would walk behind the horses, maybe thinking of home where our mother was waiting for us, sitting in the doorway knitting socks or sweaters,[15] and looking toward Punquiqasa Peak where travelers from the mountains came into view, eager to see us the moment we appeared laden with fruits from our travels. Or maybe she was thinking she just wanted to see her husband and sons safe and sound. Every once in a while Papa would say: "Not much farther to Cabildo," and he would stuff a wad of coca leaves in his mouth.[16]

At that time, Shining Path was expanding; everywhere you went they were talking about social justice. On the radio we heard young people and professors talking about a people's war. Our parents and others said: "The organization is already here" (kaypiñas kachkan partido) or "They say they have killed over there" (wakpis wañurachinku).

Auquiraccay is the town where I was born. When we were very little our parents took us to live in the community of Killa, on the banks of the Apurímac River. And that is where we established our permanent home.

A week before we had planned to return to the forest, on a market Sunday in January 1983, I traveled with my uncle from Auquiraccay to Nuñunga, to that village's market. I bought canvas shoes there, and a few other things I needed. On the way back, we came upon my brother's friend Raúl.[17] They had studied together at the school in Mayu. I asked about my brother, and Raúl said he was far away, fighting for social justice. He was headed to the forest and would be returning a week later because the Communist Party leadership had given him permission to visit his family.

Soon dusk came to Auquiraccay. We spent that afternoon with Raúl at my uncle's house. The next day, as I accompanied Raúl to a certain point—because he was headed to the rain forest—he said that if I wanted to see my brother I could join him on his way back. And that is what I did.

I have always remembered that day when I left my community of

Auquiraccay, when I left my aunt's house.[18] With her eyes full of tears she pleaded with me to stay. But I had made up my mind, convinced. I embarked on an unknown adventure, with no idea when I would return. I was twelve years old.[19]

That day there was a heavy mist in the heights of Auquiraccay. Auquiraccay always made me remember my childhood, because that's where I studied first grade. I remember that the teacher cut our hair short like the army recruits. Along with my companions, I learned my vowels under threat of the whip. In the school patio we learned to stand up straight and sing as loud as we could: *We are free, we will always be free.* We repeated those words mechanically, without any idea what they meant. I attended that school for three months; then we went back to the forest. That was what life and school were like back then.

How many things you can remember just by looking at the town! But that misty day I stood near the heights of Auquiraccay, where the paths crossed, by the cemetery. Nostalgia swept over me as I thought of when I played with my friends, tumbling around in the green grass as we watched over our sheep and pigs.

I waited impatiently for Raúl, who was coming from the rain forest after visiting his parents.[20] We were supposed to meet in the morning. What if he hadn't shown up? I might have returned home, and my history would have been different. But Raúl soon appeared, his pack (qipi) on his back. We greeted one another and began walking to the community of Cochas, where we thought we might find his squad.[21]

We walked all day. Around five in the afternoon we were approaching the Cochas Valley. We could see people with sweaty skin, on their way home from their fields, hauling their animals and tools. Some people recognized Raúl and called out: "How are you *compañero?*" (Allinllachu compañero?) *Compañero*, or comrade, was the new word people called each other, instead of uncle, grandmother, father or brother.

The local squad was not in the town; Raúl was told it was probably in Huallay. We spent the night in the community of Mayu, in the home of an old woman. She lived on the main road that led to San Miguel and other places. The old woman made us a potato (chuñu) soup and we sat outside the kitchen (tullpa) to eat. She asked us where we were from. We told her we came from the rain forest.

Early the next morning we continued our search for the squad. Mayu was a valley filled with green; it is still like that because of its geographical location. It has fruit trees and hundreds of birds flying this way and that, in endless celebration.

We walked along a fence whose posts were plum trees. Yellow passion fruits hung from vines that crawled among their branches. When we passed close to a particular house, someone Raúl knew called out and invited us to have squash soup made with curdled milk and some herbs I had never tasted in my life. It was awful and I thought I was going to throw up. During the entire trip, Raúl would give me looks I knew were meant to teach me how I must behave in my new life in the Peruvian Communist Party, how to greet people and the duties I would have. He told me that when someone invited us to a meal I had to finish it gratefully. And so I did. Later, continuing our journey we came to a river whose waters were high and turgid. We crossed it with great difficulty and then began to make our way up a steep incline.

As we walked, Raúl told me: "In the party each member has a special name." And so I had to choose my combat name. My brother, when we used to fish in the Apurímac River that ran gurgling along one side of our house, would talk to me about Che Guevara, and he also gave that name to our little raft.[22] So I told Raúl I would take that name. "I don't think that will work. Why don't you call yourself Carlos; it's the same as Che Guevara." The name Carlos accompanied me until 1995.[23]

Around noon we came to a town called Llachuapampa, where we found a group of women crying and protesting that soldiers had raped them and taken their hens. All of a sudden we heard gunshots. Before the soldiers saw us, we ran into a gorge. When we were sufficiently far away, we stopped to rest by the side of a wheat field. A woman with small children was weeding the field. We greeted her and said we were *compañeros*; she understood and invited us for some *mote* with *charki*. She said: "Poor things, look where you are!"

Two hours later we were at the top of Mount Tankar. In the distance a dark green helicopter flew across the blue sky. We came to the community of Huayanay and asked the villagers if the squad was there. They told us no: "We haven't seen any *compañeros*; they come and go without warning." Raúl was not impatient with our labyrinthine search. He remained calm. I was the one who thought maybe the soldiers had captured them. From Raúl's explanations, I learned that guerrilla life meant that you lived among the peasants, becoming one with them in time and space.

I still had 5 soles in my pocket, left over from what I was carrying to buy those clothes, and I used them to get a soda and some crackers at the store in Huayanay. Soon it was night. On the advice of some peasants we retired to the town. They told us soldiers were constantly coming by and resting in a rustic hut (*chuklla*). Peasants only used that hut when they were out with their animals.

Around noon the next day we headed to another town, Huallay. Someone had told us we might find the squad there. We walked almost all day long. Late in the afternoon we made our way down through a grove of eucalyptus and fruit trees. Ahead of us appeared a little adobe house with a roof of grass (*ichu*). "They are in that house," Raúl told me, "when we arrive we will say hello, and I will introduce you." The sun was dying on the horizon, tinted red like the Communist Party flag.

At last we had found the local forces squad. The house was closed up, but the guards on watch recognized Raúl. There were about thirty guerrillas there, most of them young people between the ages of eighteen and twenty-five.[24] Half were women. They seemed happy, singing guerrilla anthems accompanied by guitars; their fingers moved passionately across the strings. We greeted each of them. Raúl introduced me as Rubén's brother; that was my brother's name. Everyone looked at me.

A few hours later they served dinner in one large bowl that contained fresh corn soup with cheese. An anecdote I will always remember from that evening is that after they passed me the bowl of soup I kept on eating from it, thanking them as I did. The *compañeros* looked at me. When Raúl told me to pass the bowl on to the person next to me, I understood that in this new way of life everyone ate from the same bowl.[25] When we finished eating we sang guerrilla songs:

Through the valleys and the Andes free guerrillas roam,
we are the best fighters of countryside and city.
Neither pain nor misery will cause us to give up,

we will keep going without ever turning back,
we will keep going without ever turning back.
Our people command us to fight until victory,
onward comrades, our motto is to win,
onward comrades, our motto is to win.
In the final battle we will defeat fascism.
Down with imperialism! Down!
Long live our freedom![26]

When it was time to sleep, the person in command, who wore an army uniform (black boots, dark green pants, and a black shirt—back then, because it wasn't always like that),[27] ordered us out onto the patio so they could rearrange the room. Then, one by one we went back in, taking off our shoes as the political leader instructed: "Get in line."

We would lie on our sides in jackknife style, alternating women and men like the fronds of a palm tree.[28] Our superiors slept at each corner of the bed. We could hear the complaints: "Straighten your foot, compañero!" (Compañero chakkita estiray!) "Compañero, your knee!" (Compañero chay muquykita!)

Later the military leader would tell us to sit up, and before we slept he would say: "In the name of Leninism, Maoism, and Chairman Gonzalo, if our miserable enemies should come and surprise us, we will divide ourselves in the following way: the men on guard[29] will stay close to me; the rest will go out two by two, everyone in silence; the contact point will be the highest nearby point (puna). Tonight there are three surveillance groups. Three people will stand guard for an hour, two together and one making rounds. Kitchen detail will get up at four in the morning. Any questions? Good night, compañeros."

This was how the military leader would instruct us, and this was the way it was every night that I was with the Peruvian Communist Party. Being organized was a necessity for the guerrilla troops. To be prepared to go on or die. Approximately forty people slept in a small room made of adobe and stone, with a grass roof. That first night I hardly slept because of the discomfort and changing of the guard that rotated hour by hour and woke me up. Later I adapted to the life.

At four in the morning they told us the soldiers were coming; we were totally disorderly getting out of that hut. Our shoes were everywhere, and we grabbed whichever ones we could reach. The soldiers weren't really coming; it was just one of the military leader's drills, to see if we were ready for war and also, I am sure, for the benefit of the newcomer who had just become a member of the red army.

The first time I did guard duty was with Rosaura. That was my first experience; after that I did thousands, and I don't remember who I did them with. That first time our shift was from midnight to 1 AM, which is when the healer (hampiq) in my village gets up to call the soul of a sick child. We had to keep our eyes wide open and our ears attentive; we talked the whole hour, and among other things she told me that this struggle would end one day but that there were reasons to fight, and she encouraged me in this path I had chosen. "We must always be ready and prepared for death" (listollañam kana wañunanchikpaq), she said, because no one here lives forever. At any moment we could be shot or tortured by the military or the village militias (ronderos).

MY FIRST EXPERIENCES IN THE RANKS OF SHINING PATH

We were watchful twenty-four hours, hungry, cold, in the rain or extreme heat. Guard duty at night was always exhausting. We might fall asleep and our enemies surprise us. And so, at night there were always four of us keeping watch when we were in strategic areas, as well as a fifth who made the rounds of the various posts. By day, we kept vigil at more distant spots, preferably high up where we had a broader view.

At dawn that day we ate a soup much like the one the night before. Then some read from the few books we had by Marx and Mao's *Five Essays on Philosophy*. The other children and I understood little of what we heard. All we saw were red letters with drawings by Chairman Gonzalo. Other *compañeros*, in small groups, went out to obtain food in the nearby communities. That was the guerrilla's routine: read, sing, have discussions, find food, and be ready for combat.

On another day the soldiers showed up around three in the morning. We left the hut and retreated to the highest reaches of Huayanay. The soldiers came from the military base at San Miguel, four hours away. That day we suffered hunger because we were unable to prepare a meal.

Night came. We climbed even higher, to a peasant community deep in the mountains. There people organized by the party offered us shelter and food. We cooked the geese and potatoes they gave us, and we rested.

The next day, after a breakfast of wheat soup with potatoes and peeled broad beans, the leaders gathered us together and told us that we would be going out in groups to obtain food from the nearby villages. We were to say that we had come in the name of the party and they would give us what we wanted. We did this every time we arrived in an area, and the peasants, who were our support base, were familiar with the activity. We guerrillas were like the Franciscan brothers who wore sandals or rubber boots and carried a small bag or lliklla on their backs for all their earthly goods: a notebook and jacket, nothing more.

An hour later we descended a steep canyon and split up in every possible direction in order to reach the houses that were scattered across the landscape. Below us hung transparent waterfalls that originated in the heights of the coldest peaks. Clouds floated about us. As we walked, Rosaura asked me a lot of questions, just like that time when we were on guard duty together: had I been studying, why had I joined up, if I missed my people.

Long after bullets destroyed her womanly figure—later I will tell how that happened—I still remember her smile and her big deep eyes. She was seventeen back then, and I was twelve. It was the month of February 1983. She knew my brother Rubén. And she always told me: "You look a lot like him." (Kaqllañam kanki.) Now we were squatting beside the little stream whose fresh cold water came bubbling down from the heights. It was hot so we wet our heads. "Why are you here?" she asked me again. "I came because of my brother," I answered.

Moving on, we arrived at the first house. When we called at the door, after the dogs began to bark an old man emerged followed by two barefoot children. We greeted them in the name of the party and asked for their collaboration. They treated us with kindness, giving us potatoes and beans. We thanked them and went on to the next house. We walked among eucalyptus, willows, and walnut trees, and then continued along the edge of fields sewn with corn, potatoes, and peas. Many birds were in the air: parrots, thrushes, tuya, chiwaku, kestrels.[30] Nature smiled at life; there were still many reasons for the cactus to bloom among its thorns. And we too had reasons to go on living.

Around midday, we rested in the grass beneath some eucalyptus trees. An endless horizon opened out before us, a green landscape with multicolored flowers. It was the rainy season. There was a cloudless sky, and a solitary sun in the universe. Below us the river snaked through canyons, and in the distance we could make out a patch of grazing sheep. On the other side of the river we could see peasants clearing their wheat fields. Around three in the afternoon, loaded down with foodstuffs, we got back to where the rest of our *compañeros* were waiting.

Very early the next day we moved on to the town of Tankar. During the day, the guerrillas always moved in twos, keeping a kilometer's distance between each pair. Thanks to this tactic, we always survived ambushes; sometimes the first few or those in the middle would be caught in the attack, but the rest managed to escape. The army, on the other hand, always marched in columns, so it was easy to ambush them.

Once in Tankar, we slept until the sun had disappeared behind San Miguel Peak. At five in the afternoon our commanders ordered us to set out for the community of Mayu. They reminded us that we were at war.

That night it was darker because of the black clouds covering the sky. We didn't walk two by two but all together in a single column like the soldiers. No one spoke. All we heard were the screeching of crickets and croaking of frogs. Walking like that was uncomfortable. All of a sudden our leader stopped us and whispered: "We're going to attack that house and kill the miserable bastards; everyone surround the house." I felt fear because it was the first time I would witness death. We circled the house, the chosen ones entered,[31] we heard revolver shots, and I saw a man run out in agony while a woman screamed in back. "Get him," the leaders ordered. We hit him with sticks and stones and kicked him. He was on the ground, pleading for the sake of his children that we not kill him.

The military leader handed a rifle to comrade Sandra so she could shoot the man in the head. She shot straight and finished him off. "This man is a rat, a *yanauma*," our leaders told us.[32] I felt even more afraid.

The other *compañeros* were calm. The night turned black, shadowy, sad, and melancholy. A few rapacious owls flew off at the sound of the shot.

Our goal was to eliminate the *yanaumas* in the peasant communities. And so, our visit to the community of Tankar was not for pleasure. Our leaders, with their "thousand eyes and thousand ears,"[33] had learned that two people in that community had been going to the San Miguel military base to tell the soldiers our whereabouts. And those people had to be eliminated right away.

We walked a few hours more, slipping and sliding in the February mud. We didn't find *yanaumas* in the other two houses. Some *compañeros* remarked: "The sound of the shot scared them off, but they will fall." Soon we could hear the Mayu River. It was around three in the morning. We had to cross that tumultuous river, rumbling and growling beneath us, on a single eucalyptus trunk. When it got light, we marched up to Mayu again and slept the rest of the day.

CARNIVAL TIME, 1983

Carnival came, as it came to my village every February, just as we were taking control of the support bases around San Miguel.[34] The customs were similar to those in my village, and the party had said we could go. We sang as we walked from community to community, cutting *yunsa* trees, and belting out traditional songs.[35]

Chayraqmi, chayraqmi
chayayhamuchkani compañeros,
wayrallawan, vientollawan parischakuykuspa
was! was!

The villagers of Mayu and Cochas welcomed us, with *puchero*, a typical dish prepared for carnival with beef, pork, peaches, sweet and regular potatoes, and tender corn. We had talcum powder and dirty water fights. In the afternoons we danced around the tree singing "I am only now arriving, now arriving . . ." (chayraqmi, chayraqmi chayayka-muchkani . . .). The Peruvian Communist Party leadership always cut down the tree.[36] This was why there would be no tree the following year, because the party cadre was likely to have gone somewhere else, or might have died in combat.

Informants had to be exterminated. And there was no lack of them in every village we visited. Others died even though they were innocent, because of quarrels among the villagers. Someone would accuse them of being informants, and the leaders would order their capture. Some of these people we discovered dancing at the carnival *yunsas*; drink made them reveal what they had told the military. Right there we would take them away, and kill them later that night. No one witnessed this, only the dark canyons, the cold waters that descended from the heights of Mayu, and the Andean broom plants (*retamas*).[37]

One afternoon our leaders took us to harass the soldiers at San Miguel. We left after eating stew. It was a long way, and we got tired. It took us four hours to get there. Around midnight we were at the entrance to the base, yelling: "Fucking bastards, long live Chairman Gonzalo! Get up and fight us face to face! Damned reactionaries, soon you will all die! Why do you listen to that bloodsucker Belaúnde?"[38] They responded with machine-gun fire and grenades. The bullets crisscrossed the dark space like shooting stars, only to lose themselves in the night. We stayed on the ground until the gunfire stopped.

We always harassed the soldiers like that. That was our strategy. Week by week, or maybe once a month, we would show up at different military bases. That night we came back happy, saying we had made the repressors mad. Those bloodsuckers: it would not be long before they left our village.

One rainy afternoon in March, Rosaura left our column together with two other comrades. They were headed for a guerrilla base in the heights of Churcampa (Huanta). It was sad when someone left, and sadder when it was someone with whom you could share your feelings. All she said was: "Take care, Carlos."

JOINING THE MAIN FORCE

We were in the community of Tankar when a Shining Path comrade arrived. He was of medium height, serious, with a weapon on his shoulder. He brought fraternal greetings from comrades on the other side of the mountain (the heights of Huanta district). He belonged to the Main Force, Company 90. Later he met with our political and military leadership, commanders of the Local Force who operated in the peasant communities of San Miguel. Around midday they informed us that Company 90 needed reinforcements because it had suffered a number of dead and wounded. My name appeared among the many who were chosen. That very afternoon we set out toward the cold mountains of the district of Tambo. We said goodbye to our *compañeros*. They were sad, and a few of them cried.[39] Out of fifty, twenty of us had been chosen: nine women and eleven men. It took us two nights to get to where Company 90 was camped. What I most remember was crossing Challhuamayo River; the water was so cold. We had to take our clothes off in order to cross. Naked, we made it to the other side, and then hiked up to the highway that goes to San Francisco (in the Ayacucho rain forest). Every once in a while a car would pass. By midnight we were in Guindas. We rested at the home of a comrade. It was just for a little while, then we continued on. That night was long and the route was too.

Rubén, which was the pseudonym of my brother, who by then was eighteen years old, was studious, critical, and rebellious. When he went off to do his obligatory military service in Ayacucho, he had already picked up the ideas of the Peruvian Communist Party. He never told us how he hooked up with the guerrillas.

One afternoon he left the house. He said he would be back soon, that was all. We cried when he left. Papa spent hours looking toward the pathway where he thought he might reappear. He looked down at his coca and said: "Maybe he is dead, or maybe he'll come tomorrow."

When I found him, he was wearing an *Iquichano*, a poncho worn by someone from the highlands of the village of Iquicha, and a woolen cap (*chullu*).[40] He had a revolver in his belt. He looked serious and thin. We only talked a few minutes. He asked about our father.

There were a lot of people in that place called Rumi. They came from all over, and from that place too they departed for wherever the superiors decided they must go.

I was ordered to Company 115, operating in Ayahuanco (a remote district in Huanta province). I told my brother that was where I was headed. All he said was: "We will meet again." And so I understood that, beyond our brotherly sentiments, obedience to the party came first. Go where you are sent and offer your life in the name of the Peruvian Communist Party. Your name would remain forever engraved in collective memory. You would be a guerrilla hero.

I was sitting there, sad, trying to understand the party's decisions, watching the comrades greeting one another and saying goodbye. At that moment one of Rubén's comrades, one of the high command, told me to stay.

And so, thanks to that comrade I stayed. And I am still alive. Because all of my *compañeros* who set out for Company 115 would be assassinated by the village militias (*ronderos*) in Yawarmayu, at the heights of Huaychao.

That Company 90, of the Main Force, had three squads, each made up of fifteen or thirteen people, men and women. It had a variety of weaponry: automatic rifles; several revolvers caliber 22, 38, and 48; double-bore rifles; old Mausers; and bombs made from soda cans. This was good, because when we arrived in a community the people would feel protected by our arms.

We went from community to community, from masses to masses, throughout the district of Tambo and the heights of Huanta. We almost never stayed more than three days in one place. We only traveled at night. We were supposed to study those books by Lenin, and Gonzalo's pamphlets, as much as we could. We ate little, once a day, but sometimes there was a lot of food. Normally in 1983 we had our three square meals: potato starch soup, corn, barley, vermicelli, and sometimes more complex dishes such as noodles, *pucapicante*, or green meat with *mazamorras*.[41] Later we only had two meals a day, and by 1985 we ate only when we found something to put in our stomachs. My brother was sent to another group in the territorial zone, where months later, following in his footsteps, I was also sent.[42]

YAWARMAYU *RONDEROS*

Our leaders always reminded us that the people of Yawarmayu had rebelled against us, that they were loyal to the army, and so they were traitors (*yanaumas*). For this reason we had to eliminate the highlanders (*chutus*), make them disappear. The day we attacked Yawarmayu there were three hundred of us, including women and men from the communities, and those from around Tambo: Guindas, Rosales, and other villages.

We set out one winter afternoon in 1983, headed toward the community. It took us two days to get there. We only walked at night; by day we slept in the caves. People joined us, coming from the different villages.

Around four in the morning we had surrounded the camp belonging to the village militia (*ronderos*) of Yawarmayu. It was located on a high hill and was strategically defensive. Soon it began to get light. Protected by our guards, we started launching stones with *waraka* (a kind of slingshot). They did not have arms, only knives. We killed one of their guards with shots from our Mauser. When we reached their camp we saw how the village militia had fallen and rolled down the hill, decimated by our bullets, some of them decapitated. We burned all their shacks. There were bodies everywhere. Along with us, the peasants who had joined us from the different villages took everything they had. Then we began our return journey.

It was not only that once, but many times, maybe five. We always had to attack those traitors (*yanaumas*), always. On other occasions we suffered casualties among ourselves.

MY BROTHER'S DEATH

The last time I saw my brother was when he came to a comradely luncheon at Company 90, just a few days before his death. We held that kind of luncheon when the leadership met, or when the Peruvian Communist Party hosted a party. It was an opportunity to get together with friends. My brother was not as thin as before. Smiling, he asked me: "Are you getting used to this?" "Yes," I told him. Then he gave me a little book with a red cover: *The Five Essays on Philosophy* by President Mao Tse-tung and a green backpack embroidered with several colors. "When I come back I will bring you a pair of canvas shoes," he said. He was like that, serious but kind. It always made him happy that I was part of the red army. The canvas shoes never arrived. Maybe that is why I spent my whole time in the guerrilla with rubber sandals or boots of seven lives, the cheapest they had at the markets.[43]

The day of his death it rained a little in the morning, but soon it cleared. It was June 1983. Around six in the afternoon the news of my brother's death came. I cried. Later the survivors told us in greater detail: "We were stopping cars,[44] when suddenly a convoy of marines appeared. We could not escape. Rubén ran downhill." A grenade launcher had ripped apart my brother's head. That same afternoon they buried him wrapped in a red flag. I never found my brother's grave. People only told me: "It is over there."

ERRORS AND THE DEATH PENALTY FOR MEMBERS OF THE PERUVIAN COMMUNIST PARTY

One cold winter afternoon, when we were peeling potatoes for cooking, the messenger from the Peruvian Communist Party came, as he often did, to invite us to a gathering that very night up in the community of Rosaspata, in Tambo. "You've got to come right away!" (kunan punis rinaykickich!) he told the leaders of Company 90. We left that night, under a full moon, and got there around four in the morning. There were many compañeros who had arrived from all over. It was a large meeting of all the groups in that part of the region.

All morning we rested; some cooked while others stood guard.

In the afternoon the regional political leadership called the meeting. There were more than 120 guerrillas present. We sang guerrilla anthems. Then the political chief said: "In the name of Leninism, Maoism, and the philosophy of Gonzalo, this meeting is to inform you that among us we have compañeros who have betrayed the Party and have sold out. For this reason tonight they will die." And he ordered that they be taken prisoner.

They grabbed eight guerrillas: three women and five men. They had been invited like the rest of us, but had no idea of what was going to happen to them. The condemned were between eighteen and twenty-two years old. These compañero guerrillas had been in the Party for almost a year and a half. Two of them were comrades and the rest simple guerrillas.[45] What I heard was that when sent out to collect food, medicine, clothes, and money, some of these compañeros asked for collaboration in the city and in the peasant communities but only handed over half of what they received, keeping the other half for themselves. Others overstayed their vacation time.

With their hands tied with rope woven of llama wool, they cried and begged for mercy. Forgiveness did not exist in the party. Loyalty or death. We had to strictly obey any task the party commanded and return to our village like Spartans, either with our shield or upon it. To die wrapped in the red flag was honorable. To die shot down in front of everyone was a dishonor.

After this death speech, the *compañeros* were sentenced to be shot. We descended into a gorge on that dark cold night in June. Ignoring the human pain of the prisoners, we pulled roughly on their ropes as they tried uselessly to break free. The grave was already dug. One by one we shot them. Before they died, each said goodbye as they had done so many times before, crying as they shook our hands. Some of the condemned shouted "Viva Gonzalo, viva Mao!" but some just cried in desperation.

We buried them in two graves, one body on top of another. The night grew darker.

This kind of death happened often. What I most remember is when the military leader ordered us to form a column, two by two. Then he would tell us that one of us had fallen asleep on guard. I think almost every one of us fell asleep at one time or another. Was this a crime? For the party it was. It was written in the imaginary rulebook. The person had to die. No one but the leader knew who he or she was. No one could protest; we did not have that right. Our political leader said: "If I touch you on the shoulder as you pass by, you are the one who can no longer exist within the Party." And we would begin to move with a Russian military step and our heads held high, nervous, awaiting that deadly tap — like Jesus's apostles waiting to see who would receive the piece of bread soaked in betrayal.

A few minutes later, a fifteen-year-old adolescent received the touch of death. His hands tied, he was shot without being allowed to say a word. We buried him by the stream that flows down the eastern side of Mount Razuhuillca.

An execution also took place one afternoon when we had just returned from attacking and looting a community near Tapuna. We had gotten lots of canned tuna, crackers, and candies.

Compañera Martha had stolen a can of tuna fish and three crackers before going on guard duty. A comrade turned her in to our leader, and that very night she was sentenced to death. As always we were seated together, one candle dimly illuminating our faces. Petty thieves were not supposed to exist in the Party, but we were allowed to steal from the peasants.

Our leader asked us how we thought Martha should die. Each of us had to answer: shot, strangled, stoned, hanged. "And you, how do you want to die?" he asked Martha. She did not answer. And so they strangled her with a length of rope. We could not bury her because we were retreating. And we did not have a pick or shovel to dig the grave. So we left her in an abandoned house, a house without a roof, eaten by time. A few days later when we passed that way again, dogs were fighting over her putrefied flesh.

Compañera Fabiola was the one who died most dramatically. She was cooking when we came and told her the leaders needed to see her. "Sit down," she said, but with the phrase "go on now" we remained standing. She was a good person. When she cooked, all the food tasted fine. As we sat around in the afternoons she would delouse us. She washed our clothes when it was her turn. But she was condemned to death. What was her crime? Without permission, she had taken an extra week of vacation and, worse, had fallen in love with a policeman in Tambo. The leadership had found a piece of paper in her pocket, on which the police sergeant had written that they would meet at the end of the month. She cried that day in front of the company that condemned her to death. They left her tied up all afternoon. No one went near her. No one spoke to her. Only among a few intimates did some of us dare to whisper "poor thing."

That night we hanged her. Five of us were ordered to do the deed. She was strong. It took us almost half an hour because she would not die. At last we buried her. The next day, the grave where we had deposited her was empty. They called the person in charge of putting her to death, and he insisted that he had hanged her until she had no more breath. But they told him one more error and they would shoot him. We found Compañera Fabiola's body in the gorge. She must have regained consciousness and, in her desperation, fallen into the abyss. Something incredible, we said. "Bad plants never die," said the comrades.

AMBUSH AT RUPARUPA

In the spring of 1983 we went to Ruparupa, in the high part of the Ayacucho rain forest. We had been practicing with explosives, learning how to blow up military vehicles. When the sun disappeared between the western hills, we descended the Guindas gorge, singing our anthem, "The Motto":

Today's motto is to conquer support bases.
For this we are willing to give our lives.
You of the earth, shaped by sky,
with the force of our weapons we build a New State.
Conquering the bases we will make that new State,
constructing the future with our blood.
Our war demands that we conquer support bases.
By the light of the Party we will be conquerors,
with conquerors' minds.

We were twenty-five guerrillas guided by our leaders, both political and military. We got there in three days, after crossing cold gunbarrel-shaped mountains.

We camped near the Ruparupa River, a few kilometers from the highway that goes to San Francisco. Our goal on this trip, as on others, was to attack the military vehicles headed toward the rain forest or toward Ayacucho. To this end we had buried a bomb on the highway; it was connected to a battery by a cable. If a vehicle passed, by joining the wires on the battery the bomb would explode and those of us who were closest would finish off anyone left alive. Finally we would appropriate their weapons. That was the plan.

Days passed. No military vehicle appeared, only commercial cars and trucks. We were tired and had no food left. So we began stopping the cars and asking for collaboration. Those coming from Ayacucho gave us fish, bread, and rice. Those coming from the rain forest gave us fruit.

The last car we stopped that afternoon had two plainclothes policemen in it. When they saw who we were, they began to shoot. We responded and killed them both. They were carrying boxes of munitions, uniforms, helmets, short boots, and cans of food.

Around nine that night we returned to our camp, content, singing guerrilla anthems, and eating the policemen's ready-to-eat meals (*rancho frio*).[46]

CELEBRATING VICTORIES AND FESTIVITIES

In the Peruvian Communist Party we celebrated holidays, but in line with our economic possibilities. There were times when we would get drunk on beer, but on other occasions we drank alcohol mixed with water and sweetened with burnt sugar. We would also celebrate after a successful ambush against the military, or on a guerrilla's birthday, the date we initiated our armed struggle (May 17), and in observance of the victories of Joseph Stalin and Mao Tse-tung.

I think it was one cold morning in June or July when, with their guns on their backs, the guerrillas returned from attacking the police station in the town of Churcampa. Dizzy, they told stories of the attack: how they had carried it out, how the miserable reactionaries had cried, and how some of them had escaped toward the Huanta Valley. "Poor dogs, how they got away!" they said.

That day the masses slit the throats of two fat rams. We all felt an intimate joy. That was when the Peruvian Communist Party had grown a lot and was united with the peasant communities. The whole valley of San Miguel, Tambo, Huanta, and Ayacucho supported the party. Word came down from the Central Committee that in 1985 we would take the city of Ayacucho, the Yankee capitalists would leave our country, man's exploitation of man would be a thing of the past, and we would live in a land free of humiliation with food enough for everyone. No longer would there be rich and poor. The peasants would lead our nation's destiny.

This is how we talked, and the peasants repeated those phrases. For all of this, and because of our victory at Churcampa, we needed a fiesta. We deserved it. Beer flowed from glass to glass. "Long live the Party!" "Viva!" we echoed. "Long live Chairman Gonzalo!" Compañero Guillermo, who played the guitar, could make us cry with his songs: "Pichiw, waychau qanmi yachanki wañunayta . . ." (dearest one, you know when I must die . . .). We young ones got dizzy quickly. Not all of us got drunk; our leaders always chose four guerrillas, and one of them had to be a comrade. They stood guard; they could only drink a few glasses of beer, nothing more. That was how it was.

This time some drank so much they fell asleep on the ground. Others went off to have sex with their lovers, behind the house or out among the rocks that were abundant in the area. But those who had sex did so in private, since it was forbidden to engage in sexual relationships, much less get married. How would a pregnant woman be able to run if the soldiers suddenly appeared? What's more, as guerrillas we were blood brothers, loyal to the party until death. Still, as monks say, man is of flesh and bone. We were too.

VILLAGE MILITIA (*RONDEROS*) OF YANAMAYU

At the beginning of 1984 we attacked the village militia of Yanamayu. We were approximately 150 at the time, all from the communities around Tambo. We set out by night from the heights of Ccarhuapampa. By eleven, we were coming down into the community. We entered in three groups and surprised their guards. Gunfire from FALS (automatic rifles) began to sound,[47] and we could hear a few screams. Alerted by the sound of automatic gunfire, we began to hear whistles here and there. We could make out people shouting for help. Soon the houses began to go up in flames. The attack lasted almost an hour. Then we began to board the return vehicle. Even far away we could still see the houses burning. "We killed some ten traitors," the *compañeros* said. As always, the indigenous members of the support bases and we guerrillas came back loaded down with all that we had looted from the houses. This was what our superiors ordered us to do: confiscate weapons, food, and clothing.

TAMPI MILITARY BASE

In the winter of 1984 we went with more than two thousand to the military base at Tampi, determined to ambush the military and eliminate it from the zone. It took us five days to get there, walking from the heights of Tambo. The people, all peasants, joined us along the way. We traveled only at night. By day we slept in peoples' houses, hidden from view. We took the route through Huayao, Huayanay, and Chaca. We attacked the military installation around midnight. Torches made from rags soaked in kerosene lit the whole of Mount Tampi. Immediately we began firing on the barracks.

Our goal was to surprise the soldiers with our numerical superiority and push them toward the precipice. But they responded with automatic firepower and forced us to retreat. We were exhausted by sleeplessness and hunger. Where would so many people find food? We had consumed our toasted corn. We arrived in Anchihuay and cooked root vegetables and potatoes. I got sick there; I could not keep on walking. I told myself: "I will stay here and catch up with the group tomorrow."

"You cannot stay," they told me. So the *compañeros* took turns carrying me on their backs. The masses returned to their communities.

COMMUNITY OF TINKA

At this time I belonged to the group called territorial forces. This group was in charge of searching out and recruiting new volunteers, and of coordinating with the communities in order to buy provisions in the city. My brother died belonging to the territorial forces.

From time to time we would meet with the masses. Everyone showed up on time, no one could miss the appointment. If they did it would cost them their lives, for the crime of irresponsibility and failure to obey the party.

Once I had to go to a community by myself. It was so I could inform the people about some missions we had to carry out. No one was supposed to know where we were going, not even us. We only had to say that the party needed their support on such and such a date, and that ten people from this community would be required. Other communities provided other types of support.

That night, when I entered the house, everyone was sitting around enjoying (*chakchando*) coca.[48] One of the leaders greeted me. I sat before them and made the entrance ritual—as we always did—saying: "In the name of Marx, Lenin, and Chairman Gonzalo." I don't remember what else I said. I did not know what to say, only that we were fighting for social justice, but in Quechua. When the meeting ended, I heard murmurs: "How is it possible that they send a child," they were saying; "They should send someone older."

We walked through the night to the community of Tinka. "These village militia *ronderos* are tough," said our leaders. When we approached the community, the guards became aware of us and began to shoot. Those of us who were in position to do so returned fire. Between the sounds of gunfire, the village militia of Tinka awoke. They shouted: "Kill those terrorists!" We did not kill anyone. We retreated with a few wounded on our side.

COMMUNIST MARKET IN RUMI

After weeks of anticipation, the guerrillas who worked in the territorial forces squad were told to inform the base communities that we would be holding a communist market. This is the way all future commercial trade would be. That day we raised the red flag with the hammer and sickle in the schoolyard at Rumi. People came from all over. The merchants sold bread, clothing, drink. There were three groups watching over the market, in case of trouble. All afternoon they played soccer. The price of each item was set by the party leaders. Most of the goods were traded.[49] From time to time we sang guerrilla anthems, as the red flag embossed with the hammer and sickle flew beneath a blue sky and resplendent sun. From time to time, at one corner of the playing field, while our *compañeros* played ball we would sing:

> We are the initiators of the peoples' war,
> forming detachments, carrying out actions.
> Gonzalo brought the light,
> taking from Marx, Lenin, and Mao
> he forged the purest steel.
> The masses cheer the organized rebellion,
> the actions that speak with firepower.
> Gonzalo brought the light,
> taking from Marx, Lenin, and Mao
> he forged the purest steel.
> Tearing down old walls
> dawn breaks optimistic
> and overflowing with enthusiasm.

CURING THE WAR WOUNDED

One afternoon Tania arrived at Company 90. She was a Peruvian Communist Party nurse, and she came from another guerrilla group that was operating in the district of Chungui in La Mar province. It was during the dry season of 1984, and the time of extreme violence was beginning. Days before Tania's arrival we had suffered attacks by the Yanamayu village militia. She was tired; there were no other nurses who had studied medicine. They served her supper and she slept until the following day. Before dawn, our political leader told me to accompany her because in another village, another support base, there were masses among the wounded and the nurse there needed help.

Nurse Tania had been born in Arcángel and before joining the Peruvian Communist Party had worked at the medical post in that city. There were many wounded who needed attention. The village militia of Yanamayu had used hand-to-hand combat weapons (*armas blancas*)[50] against the nearby communities in the district of Tambo who were still with us; they were our masses.

Many peasants had died. Others were still alive, with their throats slashed. They had suffered a lot of injuries. As Tania's helper, I handed her gauze and hydrogen peroxide, and she cleaned the wounds. We had to tell the wounded that they would be all right soon, that it was not serious. Furthermore, that this struggle was for social justice, for the party. Never anything different.

From that day on, I was Tania's helper. Together we walked from community to community, from squad to squad, curing people. Wherever night found us, we would sleep—in gorges, cold mountain passes, or in welcoming peasant homes surrounded by human warmth. Tania knew a lot about traditional medicine; she cooked many healing herbs. I knew some of the aromatic plants, like *yawarsunqu*, which is good for causing wounds to close and for fighting the ills that come from cold. We used *chilca, molle, cabuya* or *muña*.

In November 1984 we visited Squad 15, or maybe 14, that had come over from the district of Chilcas. We treated some bullet wounds and a few people who had flu. Because it was All Souls' Day, they had prepared sweet rolls (*wawas*). We were only there a few hours when a messenger arrived telling us there was a *compañero* who had been shot and was close to death. That was a nurse's life, always running to where she was needed.

The wounded man was lying on the floor on a blanket; the bullets were encrusted in his face. As always, we told him it was nothing serious, that he would be better soon, that we were approaching the final stage of our struggle. He lived for two months. We buried him wrapped in the red flag in a thorny gorge among cactus, prickly pear, and agave.

The number of wounded increased; we had around twenty. Some arrived with their arms broken, others riddled with shrapnel. It became more and more difficult for us to treat them because around this time almost all the communities had begun to organize as peasant militias—as traitors. They began hunting us down. We retreated to the high forest. It was hard to carry the wounded. Their arms and legs were torn by the soldiers' bullets. We walked slowly, and when we heard the sound of a helicopter we threw ourselves to the ground.

Some of our *compañeros*, with bullets embedded in their flesh, began to emit an odor of putrefaction. Vultures began circling overhead, attracted by the nauseating stench. But these *compañeros* were still alive. They could not stand guard, but they read the Marxist books and the pamphlets by Chairman Gonzalo. Those high tree-covered mountains were always shrouded in mist. That was good, because it made it harder for the enemy to spot us. But there was nothing to eat. Sometimes we spent days waiting for deer (*viscacha*) so we could hunt them like primitive men, with stones and improvised spears. Once we trapped a deer and ate him, licking the bones until they appeared corroded by time. But other times we did not even have water to drink. Four of our wounded died; we could not bury them, nor did we have red flags to wrap them in. Those were our most difficult days.

I stopped being a nurse when they called me to a meeting at the heights of Uchuraccay. After some time, when I returned to the mist-shrouded mountains, Tania asked permission from my superior for me to stay with her, but he did not accept. That was the last time I saw Tania. Wherever she may be, I hope she is well.

PROMOTION FROM MILITANT TO COMRADE

We were at the heights of Uchuraccay when a comrade high in the organization arrived. He had four guards protecting him. He was friendly but serious. He asked us how our struggle was going. "How are you, *compañero*?" (allinmi kachkaniku compañero?) we responded. This comrade, the political leader of a large part of the region, had come to encourage us. He told us we were close to taking power, and he was going to promote some of the militant guerrillas to the rank of comrade. One of the requisites for comrade was having shown loyalty to the Peruvian Communist Party.

For a week we studied in order to be able to ascend from militant guerrilla to the rank of comrade.

Fifteen of us were candidates. I was the only adolescent. On the sixth day of that lecture we were all assembled, ready to be promoted.

The comrade arrived and, after greeting each of us in turn, he said: "I am pleased with you." (Kusisqam kani qankunawan.) Everyone was silent. It was a clear night. The candle on the wall illuminated the faces of the guerrillas, while the moon that appeared through the doorway gave the room a strange cast. Not even the slightest breeze caused the candle to flicker. All was silent. It was one of those typical nights when you just want to spend hours outside listening to the crickets screech and frogs croak. But on this night even the crickets were still. I had the impression I was skimming the pages of the books written by the comrades. The comrade in charge began to sing:

We are the initiators of the peoples' war,
forming detachments, carrying out actions.
Gonzalo brought the light,
taking from Marx, Lenin, and Mao
he forged the purest steel.
The masses cheer the organized rebellion,
the actions that speak with firepower.
Gonzalo brought the light,
taking from Marx, Lenin, and Mao
he forged the purest steel.
Tearing down old walls
dawn breaks optimistic
and overflowing with enthusiasm.

The tone of the song reverberated deep in the marrow of our bones and made us feel necessary to those who clamored for social justice. For a moment, pain and hunger faded. The ceremony ended with hugs and chants to the Peruvian Communist Party.

VILLAGE MILITIA (*RONDEROS*) OF GUINDAS

Earlier, in the community of Guindas we had been well received. Its inhabitants gave us lodging and offered their men to help us fight the forces of order, the miserable ones. They gave us their food, especially corn, peaches, and cherries in February and March. But now the community had risen up against the party; it believed in the bloodsucking reactionaries. We thought those hardheads did not understand the party's goals.

One afternoon in 1985, during the time of the rainy season (*puquy*), our leaders called for me and for my *compañero* Jorge. We were to go and make a map of the community of Guindas in order to plan our attack. They realized that we knew the community. Going there was dangerous. We had gotten used to approaching by night, and when we were on the outskirts hide and watch how people moved about. We had to make our sketch. From this sort of mission some never returned. They were probably discovered and assassinated.

That day we set out from the heights of Uchuraccay. Those peasant communities were desolate. The indigenous inhabitants had fled to the cities or into the rain forest. Only birds flew about, searching for food. The cold air of Mount Razuhuillca battered the solitary mountains, and our bodies too.

As we walked, my *compañero* said we should not go to the community because it was very dangerous. I did not want to go either, but I did not have the courage to say so. And so we stopped at an abandoned house far from the community of Guindas. There were broad beans in the garden. That night we cooked. We slept all day. That afternoon we headed back to our camp. Company 90 was waiting for us in a cave at the heights of Uchuraccay. We told them our experiences as if they had really happened.

If one of the "thousand eyes and thousand ears" had followed us, we would have died repudiated by our own *compañeros*, because seated comfortably in that abandoned house, far from the camp of the village militia of Guindas, we had made our sketch of the people's movements. We agreed never to speak of our disobedience. We kept that pact until now, because I have written it.

Four days later we attacked that community. We two were the guides. That day, thanks to who knows what, the sky was clear, there was a full moon and it was easy to see the path. I knew it well because I had been going there for months to treat the wounded. The camp was by the Guindas River. The highway to the rain forest also passed that way. There was a lot of mud. We got close to the camp. The youngest among us stood guard at a distance, listening for the whistles of the traitors. As always, we began to hear gunfire, and the houses began to burn. A few guards from the city of Tambo fired their weapons.

CRITICISM AND SELF-CRITICISM

The sessions of criticism and self-criticism took place without fail every fifteen days. These were serious gatherings meant to evaluate the behavior of the guerrillas in the ranks of the Peruvian Communist Party, a space in which to admonish or praise the combatants.

We always said the party had "a thousand eyes and a thousand ears." And so everyone knew everything. There was no use lying; you simply had to confess publicly. We were silent while each guerrilla made his or her confession. We said: "I was lazy about doing guard duty, I disrespected my *compañero!*" and so forth. It was a public confession. We never revealed the most serious errors, such as falling asleep on guard duty. The criticism would come after: "*Compañero*, you take too much time getting up to stand guard, you are still too individualistic!" The person being criticized just nodded his or her head.

TIME OF HUNGER

Some comrades said: "The Incas never lacked for food; the Spanish are the ones who brought hunger." I dreamed of great quantities of food: potato, yucca, rice, like the times when I ate sitting beside my mother. But when I woke up, all I could hear was my stomach growling. And we looked at one another like squalid dogs, but the party was there, always watching. In the party we ate from a common dish because, aside from the fact that it was our custom to eat that way, much of the time we could only find a few potatoes and water to make a meal. We sat in a circle. The *compañero* or *compañera* who had cooked served the soup in a common dish, and the person in charge ordered: "Today we are only going to eat one mouthful." That's the way it was back then: one mouthful of soup. I don't think it even reached our stomachs.

We could walk barefoot, with lice in our hair, but without eating we could not walk. And so we thought and we dreamed: when we win, when communism arrives, we will eat a lot.

When I joined the movement, we still ate well, because in every village the people prepared a variety of meals for us. Later, when they became traitors (*yanaumas*), village militia (*ronderos*), we retreated to the high sierra where there was no food. From time to time we would go down to a village to steal something to eat. Sometimes the traitors would be waiting for us, and we would return with nothing. We had become common thieves. At that time we were constantly thinking about how to steal food, confiscate weapons. That's why, when we entered the communities, after burning the houses and killing the traitors the first thing we looked for was food, then clothes. We took everything we found; it was our war booty. But we were not always able to enjoy what we looted. Sometimes they ambushed us and we ended up with nothing.

I will always remember eating horsemeat. It was a little fibrous and semisweet, but tasted good. For the people of my community, horsemeat is vile. But we needed to eat. We were not dogs or vultures, but simply starving guerrillas. In our extremity anything was good. We could not afford disgust or nausea. And so one morning we killed an old horse that had been abandoned by its owners and was roaming the hills. We cut its throat. We could see how its blood ran into the pot as we sharpened our knives on the rough rocks preparing to skin the animal. It was a joyous scene, until the helicopters arrived with their deafening rattle that terrorizes even the high mountain grasses.

The *cachicachis*—that's what we called the helicopters—began to land near our camp, probably attracted by the smoke from our cook fire. And we, in perfect formation, ran toward the mountain boulders, leaving, like so many times before, the sizzling pieces of horse skin. We had just started boiling the meat. That day we ate nothing. We spent hours thinking about that horse. That afternoon it snowed a little. Razuhuillca Peak, Apu Wamani Razuhuillca as the peasants call it, was covered in snow. We were at the height of Razuhuillca Peak, and there our meal consisted of snow with salt.

The soldiers remained in our camp and set up their dark green tent. We did not have a tent. We slept in the caves; they were our tents. We had no sleeping bags either, only grass to protect our backs, and a few dirty blankets filled with fleas and lice.

The guards informed us that more military patrols had arrived. We were situated in a strategic place; only the guards could look down from the top of the hill and see the soldiers' movements.

The military did not just stay for an afternoon. They were there for a week. A long week for us, like a long drought. At night the young guerrillas went down to look for the food we had hidden among the rocks. In the morning they returned with their bag of dried potatoes and beans on their backs. We ate the food raw because we had no pot or even wood to make a fire.

Another night, when they went down for food, they did not come back. We thought the soldiers must have surprised them, or maybe they deserted. That day we had nothing at all to eat, nor the following days. Our stomachs were empty. All we ate was snow with salt. We were thin. The *compañeros* began to cough. On the sixth day two of our *compañeros* died. Our leaders said: "We are making history," but we no longer heard their speeches. We dragged the dead men behind the rocks.

Rosaura, after two years, had returned to Company 90. She was squalid like me. Her eyes were sunken, her cheekbones stood out and her hair was ragged. Even as destitute as we were, we continued to believe in our Chairman Gonzalo, who might appear in a helicopter at any moment and do away with the soldiers. But no, he never arrived. He remained invisible.

That may be why that afternoon Rosaura told me: "Let's get out of here!" I told her I could not walk. So she made me chew on a root that grew between the rocks. That night we made it down to the military camp to turn ourselves in like repentant guerrillas. It was a long night. Every few feet we would stumble and fall. We were thinking: will the soldiers shoot us or pardon us? As far as the party was concerned, if it found us out, we were already traitors.

At dawn we reached the camp, and our rheumy eyes could not believe what they were seeing: half-opened cans of military rations littered the ground. We did not care if those leftovers were poisoned; we sat on the ground and ate. The soldiers must have left around midnight. We found parboiled potatoes. Even cans half filled with condensed milk. Rosaura returned to our party's base carrying those potatoes. She would say we had gone down to search for food since the others could no longer walk. That I, "our *compañero* Carlos," was cooking down below. Come on, eat this and let's go down. The soldiers are gone. I continued eating anything I could find.

Another time a squad of eighteen men and women went to the

heights of Calicanto, the place where the region of Ayacucho begins. We carried a number of weapons: revolvers, shotguns, pineapple grenades, and grenade launchers. Our goal was to demolish some village militia camps and detain cars in order to get food. We set out from the heights of Uchuraccay, singing the song "Belachao" ("Bella Ciao") as we took leave of our *compañeros* who stayed behind.

On a morning of radiant sun,
oh belachao, belachao, belachao, chao, chao,
on a morning of radiant sun I will hold the oppressor in my
    hands.
It is my desire to keep on fighting,
oh belachao, belachao, belachao, chao, chao,
it is my desire to keep on fighting with the hammer and sickle.
And if I die in combat,
oh belachao, belachao, belachao, chao, chao,
and if I die in combat take my weapon in your hands.
I am a Communist for life,
oh belachao, belachao, belachao, chao, chao,
I am a Communist for life, and a Communist I will die.

When we passed by the highway in Tapuna, a place we were forced to pass, we stopped a few cars. We asked for collaboration, and they gave us noodles, canned goods, and fruit. Then we continued walking, holding hands in the dark. We had been walking all night, resting now and then. When we were too tired, the older guerrillas carried us on their backs. At dawn we reached the heights of Calicanto. We slept all that day.

Over the following days, we ate all the food we had been given. Our leaders began to organize the attack on the village militia.

One night, four of the *compañeros* standing guard deserted. They left their weapons behind the door. We did not know where they had gone. Our leaders were furious; they told us if anyone thought about deserting he would be shot. Where had they gone? The army soldiers killed any deserter they found, and the village militia were eager to take revenge.

At that point there were fourteen of us left. We had a meeting to plan what we were going to do. We decided to attack a village militia at the heights of the village of Yanaorcco. A week later we entered the community. We had planned the attack several days before: we would arrive silently, avoiding the guards, and set fire to the houses with the traitors inside. And that is what we did. We were at war. We had to eliminate those who did not understand the revolution. We made off with their food. When we had gotten far away, we realized that our political leader was not with us. Had he been killed by the village militia? Months later we found out that he had deserted to the city of Huanta. We wanted to assassinate that deserter.

After a month at the edge of the jungle, in Calicanto, only six of the eighteen guerrillas who had set out from our base remained. We had no leaders, so we had to elect new ones. It was urgent. It did not take us long to choose them, but whatever the situation, we always took this task seriously and observed the lessons we had learned of first honoring the thought of Marx, Lenin, Mao, and Gonzalo, those words that guided us. We raised our fists and in loud energetic voices shouted: "Yes, compañero!" (Ari compañero!)

At that small but significant gathering, I became the political leader. Three months later I would turn fourteen. In spite of my youth and the fact that I could neither read nor write, I had reached the hierarchy. At that gathering there were people older than me, but I was the only one who was a comrade; they had no choice but to elect me. A few days later, despite the obstacles that might befall us, I made the decision to return to Company 90's base camp. I took the political leader's weapons: an automatic pistol and a lightweight HKM machine gun with collapsible stock. Each had three munitions belts. We passed over solitary mountains. Tapuna. The heights of the village of Iquicha. We walked with hunger and slept among the tall grasses that blotted out the sun's rays, and continued our journey. We could not move by day, because in the mornings the village militia came out to work their fields and returned to their bases around five in the afternoon. If they saw us, they would kill us.

We found Company 90 at the heights of Uchuraccay, right where we had left it. The Peruvian Communist Party was skeletal. That evening, seeing black clouds in the sky, we sought refuge in the caves.

PRISONER

It was during the final days of March 1985 that I fell prisoner in a military ambush, in a rocky corner of the Huanta highlands, at the foot of majestic Razuhuillca Peak.

On the morning of the day before, along with Rosaura, I had gone out to get some salt that was hidden among the rocks behind a high hill, where the deer (*viscachas*) roamed. We used to hide our food like that, because if we did not the soldiers and village militia would steal or burn it. We walked for a long way, conversing. We asked each other many detailed things, as if we were saying goodbye and would never see each other again. If those rocks could have spoken, like the peasants say, they would have told us not to continue, to go back, there is danger up ahead. But they did not speak. Sometimes hills do not speak, they are so far removed from us, like insensitive humans or our compassionless leaders.

A year earlier Rosaura had been reassigned to Company 90 and so we met up with each other again. The Peruvian Communist Party militants had to move from place to place, from one squad to another. She had known me from the time I joined the party. Rosaura always had a piece of bread with her when we went to stop cars, and when we did guard duty together we ate when no one was looking. Sometimes she thought about deserting: "We will go in May," she would say, "for my birthday." We only said these things in secret; if the comrades found out they would shoot us on the spot.

Yes, we thought about abandoning the party. It is true that the songs made us feel as if we were made of steel, but we were human, children, peasants shouting among the lifeless rocks with no one listening. "I came because of my brother," I told her. "I know," she would say, "but you did not come only because of your brother. The party needs us. Peru needs us." "I was sitting in front of my house," she went on, "when suddenly the party members entered my village. That day they killed the president of my community."

We told each other so many things as we chewed on roots in those high mountains, or when it was our turn to stand guard. Other times we would climb the highest peaks searching for the sweet greenish-black berries that hung from the trees. She kept on talking: "My father

Razuhuillca Peak, the place where I fell prisoner. Photograph by Moner Lizano, 2002.
Used by permission.

died in a military ambush. One afternoon I cut school; I came to join up with this ghost that roams the world, the ghost of communism."

By this time we were hungry, and when we were on our way back down, after getting the salt, we saw a group of *compañeros* coming from stopping cars. We caught up with them. They were cooking beans and fresh corn on the cob. We were getting ready to greet them when, suddenly, the man on guard saw that the soldiers were near. We began to run. There was gunfire, bullets coming from all directions. We were desperate. We did not want to die.

Rosaura ran beside me. A few feet farther on a bullet destroyed her arm, but she kept on running. Another bullet hit her in the back and she fell. She could no longer get up. Around us other *compañeros* fell beneath the rain of bullets. A grenade launcher exploded close by. It was deafening, and I sank to the ground. I got up and kept on running, desperate now. Pretty far away, behind a hill and exhausted, I did not know whether I was still alive. I touched my arms and only saw a few holes from bullets that had torn through my black sweater. I cried.

I made it to the camp near Razuhuillca Peak. Everyone was sad because of the death of our *compañeros*. One by one they arrived, some wounded and others frightened. It rained that afternoon, but it soon cleared. It was March 1985. We cooked potatoes and ate them with horsemeat. There were many who were wounded, or sick with tuberculosis. That afternoon, with the help of my *compañeros*, I cured the wounded for the last time. We boiled water and infused it with highland roots, and we cleaned their wounds, saying, as we had learned: "It is not serious, you will be all right soon, we will go into history as heroes."

The next morning, the guards informed us that the soldiers were approaching our camp. Soon, over our heads, a firefight started. They fired so many rounds of bullets, grenade launchers, and mortars, that the sound shook the rocks. I ran over to the sick, but there was no escape. What to do? Pretending that a bullet had ended my life, I rolled over a rock and remained face down at the edge of it. I stayed motionless like that for almost half an hour. The firefight continued. I thought of my Peruvian Communist Party, of my brother Rubén, of Rosaura who I knew was splayed on the ground in her own blood. I believed death would come at any moment. We were prepared for it, prepared to shed our blood for the party. If the soldiers had not noticed me, I would have been able to tell my *compañeros* in detail how they had passed right by without seeing me. But it did not happen like that. Chance changed the story of my life.

A soldier saw me and aimed his gun, his finger on the trigger. I did not say a word. He was shouting, saying he had found a terrorist (*terruco*). "Don't kill him," said someone farther away. Then many soldiers surrounded me and made me stand up. They took me to the lieutenant who was the chief of the patrol. They asked me many questions, translated by the village militia who were with them.[51] They were furious because they had not been able to kill us all and had not retrieved a single weapon. "We have let him live long enough," they muttered. "Let us finish him off," they said, "Kill him already!" said the village militia. I think I understood something like that.

My end seemed near. For so long I had walked, eaten or not eaten, cold and without clothes, to die like this, sad, without being able to defend myself. I was not about to cry. They told me to move a short distance away and sit on a rock. I thought about trying to run, but I would die in any case. Furthermore, I was a comrade and had to die with honor, wrapped in a red flag. I felt anger toward the soldiers and toward my *compañeros* who, possessing so many weapons, had not fired on them. I heard several shots in unison, and still I remained alive. Among raucous laughter, I heard more shots.

My eyes began to tear up. "Man, it is nothing to cry about," said those who were watching from the hill. Painfully, I swallowed saliva and breathed with difficulty. My body shook. Suddenly my eyes clouded over and I could not distinguish anything, I was so afraid that those executioners in their green uniforms and black helmets would see me. Still, I have never forgotten what I believed would be the last moments of my existence before the bullets would destroy my body. Maybe that is why I am afraid of the dark and of death. I was completely blind. A few moments more and I would be dead. I tried to shout, awkwardly, like those comrades who fell in battle: Viva Gonzalo! Viva Lenin! Viva Marx! Was this what death would be like? I thought.

My friends will know how hard it is to tell everything, but perhaps this will help them understand how my life as a guerrilla ended and another page would soon turn. When I came to, the lieutenant was talking to me, translated by some of the village militia who had accompanied the patrol. He was asking me to guide them back to the military base.

The whole way the village militia pleaded with the soldiers to kill me. In Quechua they said: "Kill that terrorist, even those as small as him have burned our houses." (Wañuchiychik chay terrucuta, paykunam, kaynachakunallam wasiykuta cañara.) But the soldiers neither understood nor paid attention.

On military patrol, 1993. Photograph by José María.

AT THE MILITARY BASE 2

Yes sir, here we are!
Soldiers,
make way,
good morning,
the Cabitos[1]
salute you.
Little terrorist,
if I find you
I will eat
your head.
One. Two.
Three. Four.[2]

Very early in the morning, formed into three columns with our military bearing, song, and rifles slung across our chests, we ran through the streets of San Miguel as the townspeople went about their daily lives. A few children followed behind, running after us for a few blocks the way dogs chase cars when they see them, as if they wanted to bite or attack.

An hour later we were back at the military base, tired of running and yelling. In short order we were taking cold showers, and then, more relaxed, we went to our breakfast of oatmeal with two pieces of bread. At eight in the morning they called roll.[3] We had to line up three deep. As they raised the flag, a bugle sounded. Immobile, standing in formation, saluting with our right hands at the height of our temples, we belted out the national anthem. Then our routine eased up. On some days we rested or played soccer (*fulbito*), but we were always required to clean our weapons and have them ready to go out on patrol.

And so, as suddenly as this, I was running with the soldiers, beginning over again, providing information. The party had denounced me, or maybe they thought I had died shouting chants to Chairman Gonzalo. Maybe the comrades had told the guerrillas: "That is how you die if you want to be wrapped in our flag!"

In the party, time was important. At seven we had a meeting. At five we examined our lives, with criticism and self-criticism. If we did not have a watch, we told time by the moon or the sun. In the army, on the other hand, the sound of the bugle marked each activity: getting up, exercising, taking our meals. "The potatoes are burning, the rice is burning," the bugle called. Even to sleep you had to wait for that bugle to sound silence.

And so, my socialist utopia dipped like the sun beneath the horizon, only to rise on a new and very different day.

After burning my ragged clothes and making me a soldier, that lieutenant, chief of patrol, who following my capture had told me to guide them back to the military base, asked me one day if I wanted to go to school.

It was right after our morning run through the streets of San Miguel. I answered immediately and with an energetic voice: "Yes, my lieutenant." That was the way you spoke in military life. He enrolled me in the primary school for boys, third grade section B. I studied there until July 1985. Every Monday, as we stood at attention in the schoolyard we recited a poem by Alejandro Romualdo:[4]

They will blow him up with dynamite.
All together, they will carry and drag him.
As they beat him, they will fill his mouth
with gunpowder. They will make him fly:

In uniform on the
Huanta base, 1986.

and they will not be able to kill him!
They will turn him on his head,
his desires, his teeth and cries.
They will kick him with all their fury.
Then they will make him bleed.
And they will not be able to kill him!

Then I listened to the applause from children and teachers, and that took me back in my memory to the little school in Killa, where for the first time I recited this poem that touched my soul. I made good grades. Later, the military base moved to the city of Huanta in order to replace the naval infantry division there. Thanks to the support of the same lieutenant, I continued my studies in Huanta. But the officers never stayed more than two to five years at the same base; they rotated. And so my military "father" left. I never saw him again. A year later, though, he sent me a Christmas package with sweets and other things.

To this point, I had no news of my family. I possessed no personal documents. A kind teacher obtained my birth certificate. From that time on, I belonged to the marvelous province of Huanta, where I was welcomed and was able to learn its customs and traditions.

For many years I continued to live at the army base called Los Cabitos Number 51. When I came of age I began my obligatory military service (*servicio military obligatorio*; SRO). That is when they begin to draft the young men of Ayacucho. After completing my military service, I reenlisted[5] as an instructor. Then I began to earn a salary.

HUANTA, THE EMERALD OF THE ANDES

In the month of August 1983, I had approached the outskirts of Huanta for the first time. I was still a member of the Peruvian Communist Party. I crossed over the cold mountains to the community of Huamanguilla. Back then we were carrying messages to another guerrilla company that operated in the Huanta Valley.

In 1985, in six military vehicles, we arrived in Huanta from San Miguel. We sat comfortably on top of blankets and tents. As the vehicle moved along, we talked about the new military base. The young recruits asked: "What will it be like? Will it have thin pretty girls?"[6] The trucks raised clouds of dust. The soldiers held their weapons at the ready, chambers loaded. Up front the officers sat beside the driver, smoking cigarettes from time to time. After five hours on the road, when we arrived at the community of Macachacra we filled our eyes with the landscape: all that exuberant vegetation bordering the Cachi River. Throughout this territory of great geographical and historical contrasts, you could read what had happened by looking at the land and, most of all, by looking at the people: a town that had suffered the violence of Shining Path, the army and the village militia, from 1980 to 1990. We identified with that song written by Ricardo Dolorier and sung by Martina Portocarrero: "On all five corners there they are/the

Sinchis are moving in/they will murder students/Huantinos at heart/ yellow, yellowing *retama* flower . . ."[7]

It was after I finished primary school and entered the convent of Saint Francis of Assisi that I learned the history of Huanta at the María Auxiliadora School. We were descendants of the oldest people in Peru. Twenty thousand years of Christ at Piquimachay.[8] Later, from 600 to 700 AD, the Warpas inhabited this part of the country, establishing commercial and cultural relations with the people of Nazca and Tiahuanaco, from whom they learned a lot: weaving, ceramics, and to work with metals such as bronze. The Waris also had a presence in Huanta, where they established a military state and conquered land as far north as Cajamarca and south to Moquegua.

This was the history of this part of the Ayacucho region. Later, commanded by Don Diego Gavilán in 1569, the Spanish established the community of Azángaro. Huanta became the capital of the viceroyalty. My Huantino countrymen were protagonists in the wars of independence. A rebellious spirit always existed, as in 1896 when they protested the law to license the extraction of salt, and in 1969 when the students demanded free education. In the 1980s Huanta lived through the upheaval provoked by internal conflict.

In 1990 I completed my third year of middle school at María Auxiliadora. In the month of October of that year, I met a lady at a wedding celebration. In mid-November, my friend Claudio and I decided to celebrate my birthday on the twenty-seventh, which is the Day of the Peruvian Infantry, at that lady's home. It is a block from Huanta's main square, a large cooperatively owned place with verandas and gardens. The party started around seven in the evening. There was a group playing guitars, a *charango*, and a harp. Beer overflowed the glasses. We were all feeling deeply happy. Friends kept arriving. By the end of the party we were almost drunk. I have good memories of that night. I met a lovely young woman and, as we talked, the street lanterns cast a weak but delicious light upon us, beneath an enormous sky.

MY LITTLE ANIMALS

I liked talking to animals, and I still like to talk to them, maybe because I was born and grew up in a peasant community surrounded by vegetation and all manner of creatures. "Take that bit of intestine," I would tell the eagle who had the habit of perching on the old oxidized tow truck at the back of the military base next to post number three.[9] That was a beautiful animal, with its black feathers, curved white beak, and sad serious gaze. The military patrols had captured it near the community of Chincho.

The fox wandered around the base with a chain around its neck. My rooster was named Koki; I would hunt crickets for him in my free time. I found them among the rocks, put them in bottles, and gave them to him to eat. On the captain's birthday they killed my Koki. It made me sad, and I was even sadder when they killed the fox. I saw the bullets embedded in his delicate ribs and *ichu*-colored feet. That fox had become a thief; it hunted the hens that belonged to a neighbor woman who lived next to the base. Those neighbors had complained more than once. One day, when I returned from my classes at the school of Saint Francis of Assisi, it was already dead. That little animal was from San Miguel. When it was small, it drank milk from a baby bottle. It was very pretty.

When I was washing my clothes in the stream that passed along one side of the base, I saw my eagle fly away. For a moment it perched on a eucalyptus branch. Then it took flight in the direction of Patasucro, a community near Huanta.

THE SEX WORKERS (*CHARLIS*)

"Here come the *charlis*, but they are old women," said the young recruits standing in the pavilion doorways. The *charlis* used to come once a week, right before we got our stipends. All coquettish, they went straight to the medical post (*tópico*) so the doctor could check them out. Their work began after evening roll call. There were always long lines. Everything was on credit, "pay later." When we got our stipends, we paid up. Some of the soldiers complained, asking "Why so many discounts?" And the treasurer always responded: "You've got a lot of nerve complaining. You still owe three tricks!" It seemed like those women had an agreement with the paymaster. But no, sometimes the sergeants visited them in a soldier's name. The *charlis* went to all the military bases and always came away happy, with lots of cash. Sometimes they would stay at a single barracks for three months.

The army also had a special anthem about the *charlis*; it is called "The Madelón." After evening roll call, we sometimes sang it proudly:

When a soldier is free in camp
with lust he goes looking for pleasure
at the tavern all covered in green
that goes by the name of Madelón.
The tavern is lively
pretty as a dream,
bubbling with fire and wine.
They all call it The Madelón.
By day in the barracks, by night in the yard,
all the while thinking of our Madelón.
If Madelón comes to fill your glasses,
you will find someone ready to flirt,
someone who will tell a joke
that will make you blush.
A good sergeant dressed to kill
went one morning to see Madelón,
in love he asked for her hand
and offer her his flaming heart.
And Madelón got right to the point:
to one man I do not belong,
for I have a whole regiment
to serve and to love.
The Madelón doesn't play favorites,
if someone tries to take advantage,
she has a smile for everyone,
Madelón, Madelón, Madelón.

Sometimes a *charli* would come with a small child, and the child played while the mother worked. Sometimes the soldiers would try to get the *charlis* drunk, and then rape them. They would complain to the captain, and at formation the commander would inform us that everyone's stipend would be docked.[10] We cursed those abusive sergeants — who did they think they were? There was always someone who threatened to kill them after they got their service leave (*baja*).

Those who came from the base at Razuhuillca Peak told us that the soldiers there had intimate relations with llamas and burros; the *charlis* did not get there very often because it was so cold.

Once our captain fell in love with a *charli*. From then on, she lived in his room. She stopped working. Some of the officers hissed under their breaths: "Let her work, my captain takes too long!"

Homosexuality also existed. A captain named Braulio would smoke dope at night and force soldiers to go with him. He took them to his room.

MILITARY BASES

There were a number of military bases. Huanta was the main one. There were others at Churcampa, Santillana, Marcas, Julcamarca, Ccayarpachi, Razuhuillca, Tambo, Ccano, Machente, and Triboline. Those who ran the bases were the captains who were members of the zone's political and military leadership. Troops and officers always rotated. The sergeants made the new recruits sing before they arrived at the bases. Those recruits did not choose where they wanted to go; they went where they were sent. It was like the party. They would tell you: "You are going over there," or "You will be staying here," and no protest was possible. It was sad, because some were picked up along with their brothers, cousins, or uncles, in Lima, Callao, or Huacho, and were separated later.[11] They might meet up again or that might be it, like the goodbye you say at the cemetery. And so, in the early morning, in some of the convoys you could hear them sing:

> Stars in the sky,
> babies on earth,
> in my heart
> the Peruvian Army.
> Sailors on the sea,
> aviators in the air
> and on earth the recruits
> with their FALs and bullets.
> The earth I tread cries for me,
> a young girl in Huanta even more.
> Passing the Ayahuarcuna bridge
> terrorists were waiting,

guerrillas were waiting for me.
Better turn back.
Triboline is sunny,
it is raining in Castropampa.
At the base where I live
are the bloodthirsty ones.
Now, now, what can you do,
it is too late now.
Buy some diapers,
buy a baby's pacifier
for the recruit.
What can you do.

For a year I managed the canteen at the Huanta base. We sold a lot, because there was no other place for the soldiers to buy what they needed. We did not have permission to go into the city. A few days before Alan García's monetary devaluation, we had spent almost all the money.[12] The canteen was full. Our sales tripled. That day we closed the canteen and kept what capital we had, without losing anything.

Once the commander ordered the soldiers at the Razuhuillca military base to come down to Huanta. The soldiers arrived with dollars. I bought 300 from them. But the commander had them line up in the yard and told them to take off their clothes. He discovered that each soldier had a stash of dollars. He confiscated a lot.

Those soldiers had attacked a commercial vehicle in transit near Toccto. I heard they disguised themselves as terrorists (terrucos). They had propaganda with them and even painted slogans on the vehicle. By luck they had ambushed a vehicle that was carrying a lot of dollars, and had divided the take among themselves. At the military base they ate like rich men, played poker, even went out to buy grilled chicken, beer, women. The truth is, the attack had been carried out by the patrol from Razuhuillca. This was discovered thanks to the owner of the vehicle, who came to the military base because he suspected that the attackers might have been soldiers, and because he was a friend of the commander. I do not know if he got his money back. They changed the personnel at Razuhuillca and never said another word about what had happened.

PRISONERS AT THE MILITARY BASE

When I arrived as a prisoner at the military base in San Miguel, there were four female guerrillas who had been trapped there by the patrols. When I entered the army installation for the first time, and passed the control post on horseback with corporal Porongo, the women were seated to one side of the kitchen pouring petroleum on the wood fire. This base was made up of two patrols of twenty soldiers each. It was headed by a major, two lieutenants who went by the names of Shogun and Savage (Salvaje), a first sergeant, two second sergeants, ten corporals, and recruits (perros) who came and went.[13]

The women cooked our food. They were young, between seventeen and twenty years old. At night they would bring them to where we slept, and they bedded down with the recruits. The sergeants took turns first, and then the rest of the soldiers until they wore them out. One of the women always slept with the major and almost never worked in the kitchen.

In the month of June 1985, one day in formation they told us to expect a military inspection. This happened every now and then; sometimes we knew in advance and sometimes we didn't. Like at our base at Huanta that time when we were caught off guard, when those three helicopters landed and we were not prepared.

For this damned inspection we had to practice marching, saluting, and making our beds with the corners properly squared. On the other hand, we had a good lunch that day, because on other days we only had tasteless army rations and some half-cooked beans. We had to tell the inspectors that the sergeants and officers treated us well, and everything was as it should be. If we did not, when the good inspectors left the sergeants would take it out on us.

Those inspectors came with their little notebooks and film cameras. They were generals, colonels, with a great entourage of other officers. It was the custom to give them gifts after they made their rounds; our own officers' promotions depended on that. In Huanta we soldiers formed a line, with baskets filled with avocados and honey that we handed to each inspector as he boarded the helicopter that would take him back to headquarters. Later we heard they had been pleased with the gifts and with the folklore presentation that we ourselves put on.

It all made them forget how badly we marched and how little we knew about combat. They gave the base a good grade.

At that time, in 1985, they decided to kill all of us who had been taken prisoner, because they were about to receive that inspection. They brought the women to where we slept, and all the soldiers had their way with them. The women cried: "Don't kill us." I was frightened too. Around twelve that night they took the women out to the parade ground where we always lined up. All of us had to witness their execution. The grave was already dug. Two shots sounded in unison and the women fell over, dead. Now it was not because they had committed an error, but because the inspection was coming and it was better to make them disappear.

I was trembling. The lieutenant who was my "father" told me the next day, when I saw the helicopter coming that I should hide. They also hid the woman who lived with the major. The helicopters arrived around ten in the morning. The inspectors stayed for three hours and then left.

A month later they caught two more members of Shining Path. They were around thirty years old. They put them in the base prison. Later they took them out and used them as guides on patrol. My friend Porongo told me they executed them in the hills.

When I got to Huanta, the naval infantry was there. They replaced it with us, the Cabitos 51. At the navy military base there was only one building with a tile roof. It had no walls. The guard posts were bunkers with mud barricades built up around them.

The day after we arrived all the sailors left. We remained. We set up tents in the fields. Around the tents we raised adobe walls. That is how we lived. I had a tuna fish can where I kept my belongings. The recruits kept theirs in bags and wooden boxes. We cooked our meals in a tow truck that had been built especially for military campaigns. The only water we had was in cisterns taken from the reservoir of drinking water at Huanta.

The prisoners were in a corral. They had been brought in by the patrol that went out to the peasant communities, and the soldiers had things that belonged to the peasants, like tape recorders, clothing, and so forth.

Some families came inquiring at the gate. They were afraid, because no civilian was supposed to set foot on a military base. The soldiers told them they had no prisoners there. That night they took them out. All I know is they said they killed them all.

A reenlisted sergeant, known by the name of Centurión, was feared by everyone in Shining Path and by the peasant militias. They all said he was a real assassin. He liked hanging the prisoners upside down and shocking them with electricity. He walked like an officer. He went out on patrol as the leader of the soldiers.

Commander Baquetón (that was the nickname by which we knew him) liked Centurión because he could trap the members of Shining Path. That sergeant ended up being condemned to death by a military tribunal because he killed an entire community.[14]

What I know is that on one occasion all the prisoners were assassinated by a military patrol.

The members of the patrol called the central base to say they were being ambushed by Shining Path. The high command informed the legal authorities—sometimes they did not even do that—and together we would go out to witness the battle between soldiers and guerrillas. The Shining Path prisoners were dead; I had already seen them at the barracks. They would place homemade bombs in their hands and strew their bodies here and there. There were about twenty dead Shining Path members lying around. They put rifles in their hands too. The public prosecutor took some notes. The police also stood around watching. The truth is, the whole scene was fabricated in order to eliminate the Shining Path guerrillas. It had happened before.

On another occasion, when we were at the Maynay fiesta, we suddenly heard gunfire. A soldier was dead, because some members of Shining Path shot him while he was urinating out among the trees, and had taken his gun. That made the commander angry; he went out on patrol all the time. It was during that time that they caught Claudio. They say he had a gun but could not escape. The commander himself captured him. When they brought him to the base they kicked him and, from a short distance, fired shots at him. Like when I fell prisoner.

Claudio was nineteen years old. They kept him in captivity and used him to help find guerrillas and retrieve arms. He did this well, and so they spared his life. He lived there at the base. Later, free, he went into the mountains of Chanchamayo. When he returned he told me he had been picking coffee. After that, back in Huanta and reincorporated into military life, he worked in intelligence with the Intelligence Service at the main base in the city of Ayacucho.

This was around the time that I was promoted to military service. When we reenlisted, Claudio went to work in intelligence at the Domingo de Ayarza barracks in Ayacucho. He was one of the best friends I ever had. On Sundays we would eat chicken at El Dorado in Huanta and get drunk together. Days before his death, when I went to Ayacucho he gave me his television, clothing and other things. He told me he would return the following Monday. We said goodbye like we always did, joking around. But he was sad. I could tell.

A few days later, news came that he had died. Members of Shining Path had killed him when he was out on patrol. A bullet went through his head and one of his legs was fractured. We mourned him at the Huanta military base. His family came. His mother never stopped crying. I gave his belongings to them. To this day I cannot accept his death, much less how he died.

In time I heard some rumors that the Intelligence Service itself had killed him. I don't know. The truth is, he wanted to get out of that kind of work. He never told me why and I didn't ask. Once I spent the night in Ayacucho at the Intelligence Service installation known as Los Gatos, where Claudio worked. Some prisoners were there, blindfolded and with their hands tied. Los Gatos asked Claudio if I could be trusted, and he nodded his head. We slept in one of the rooms. The next day the prisoners were gone. I am sure they took them to the ovens.[15] I went back to the base at Huanta.

There is another story about Chuck Norris, a child from the United States who was only seven years old. A patrol from the base at San José (in the region of Ayacucho) had picked him up. His father had died and his mother was at the Shining Path base in the village of Vizcatán. We always heard about her, especially when people came from Caja de Aguas, Lima, to Canaire in the Ayacucho rain forest. The child lived with the rest of us young recruits at the Huanta military base. They sent him to school. One day, when he went out into the street he didn't come back. The commander expelled him from the base. Years later I found him in the street. He was working at a little chicken restaurant called Tivoli, in Huamanga province. I never saw him after that.

COMMANDERS

Commanders only stayed a year at the military base. Change of command took place in January or February. The officers and petty officers received a good deal of money when they went from one post to another. Officers were always transferring between the different bases.

Every commander had a different character. Some liked to go out on patrol, others liked sports and spent their time playing basketball. One liked to farm; he brought a tractor and ploughed the whole field around the base. He made us plant carrots, cabbage and onions. Each commander had his likes and dislikes. Some liked partying and others the Olympics. One commander was mean to us. We never had another like him; he wanted everything to be done right. He made us pave almost the entire barracks area; we had to carry the rocks on our shoulders like slaves. We were tired. So, along with an experienced reenlisted man, we planned something.

It happened that around nine that night two soldiers shot a couple of rounds of bullets at the ceiling in the direction of that commander's room. "Terrorists (*terrucos*)!" we yelled. From every guard post they began shooting at the commander's room. "They're attacking us!" we said. The truth is, there were no *terrucos*. We just wanted to get back at that military monarch. The firefight lasted half an hour. Almost half the soldiers knew what was going on. The next day we did not carry rocks. Instead, they ordered us to clean our arms so we could go out on patrol. I do not think they ever discovered the truth.

MONITORS AND RECRUITS

The monitors were in charge of instructing the new recruits when they entered the military. Few soldiers forget their monitor; they remain tattooed on our memories. They always say: "That monitor of mine made me eat shit! That monitor of mine was a son of the devil!"

I too was a monitor. A senior officer taught the monitor course, which lasted two weeks. We woke up singing. After breakfast we spent the whole morning marching, practicing our turns: to the right, to the left, half turn, and diagonal. We practiced formations, columns, lines. Every morning we did basic gymnastics without our weapons (push-ups, plows, rowing, clenches, tackles, jumping jacks, vises, and pull-ups); and with them (passing them between our legs, plunging with them, moving them up and down, arching backward, twisting, and moving them in circles).[16]

One afternoon we monitors will never forget, we went out running through the streets of Huanta. With our rifles on our chests, wearing pants and half boots but without our shirts, we sang:

Yes, Sir,
the monitors
salute you,
do not fear,
they are brave
fighting men.
One, two,
three, four.

We went to the slaughterhouse and took showers amid the stench of beheaded animals. People stared at us. Some were frightened and others said: "Those are the bloodthirsty ones." And so, smelling as we did we sat down to our evening meal. Around eight that night we bathed in the cold waters of the canal that ran along one flank of the barracks. The next day we killed three dogs with our knives, and washed in their blood. Then we ate oatmeal with gunpowder. On the shooting range we lit a stick of dynamite with a long fuse. On the final day of our monitor course they made each of us drink a bottle of beer. We were fifteen monitors. Our faces were red. "Now, goddammit, you are monitors," the petty officer told us.

At the beginning of the 1990s, we were eager for the recruits from Lima and Ayacucho to arrive. The departing recruits (*perros*) told us: "Now the real *perros* are coming!" They showed up at the front gate in military convoys, all packed together like lambs or bulls on their way to the slaughterhouse. This time they were from Chimbote, Callao, and Huaraz, and from Carmen Alto in Ayacucho. There were three hundred of them, and they handed them over to us the next day. I had forty recruits in my section. That first day we cut their hair, told them how they must behave in formation in order to become Peruvian soldiers, and talked to them about the war we were fighting.

Two days later three recruits deserted. That day the newcomers didn't sleep because some of the monitors had made them eat feces in the bathroom. The complaint of mistreatment reached the commander. We all attacked the recruit who ratted, and forced him to desert. We told him loud and clear that the barracks were for real men, not crybabies.

The recruits ate as if it was their last meal. They learned that in the army they did not have their mamas there, to cool their food cooked with green wood. It was hot as boiling oil. One afternoon I got criticized because my recruits were late. Before they learned to eat fast, I ordered them to stand in formation after receiving their portions from the large pots. I told them I was going to count and they would have to have finished their meal before I got to 5. I counted one, two, three, four, five, and ordered them to turn their trays upside down. Without a complaint, my recruits threw their food on the ground. Then I said "The last to wash . . ." (the last at anything always got punished). I had gone through all that too, when I was a new recruit.

At that time in the army there was little to eat, and the young soldiers were hungry. Oatmeal soup and half-cooked beans weren't enough. We would buy bread near the guard post, where a woman sold it.

Visits were Sunday afternoon. Many families came. Before 1990 it was different; almost no one came to visit. But now civilians were allowed on base. This was a day when everyone ate a lot. In the afternoon we collected fruit; the monitors' benches were piled high with it. That night we would take the recruits to the bathroom. There was a latrine next to post number three. The recruits did handsprings as they went. Then we shouted: "To shit!" and the recruits began to run. Suddenly we ordered them to fall into line before they had finished defecating. The whole yard stank. After that, we ordered them to bathe. This was the life of the new recruit: to obey his monitor. How they hated us, but they too would forget one day—when they got promoted—and take revenge on the newcomers. In the army you followed orders with neither a murmur nor a whimper.

We monitors were not the only bad ones. Almost all the old-

timers—petty officers, lieutenants, captains, majors, and commanders were bad too. Our anthems, the military songs, encouraged us
always:

People will ask
who are the friends,
crew-cut boys,
little soldiers
with big hearts.
People say
we have no profession.
What does it matter
if they are wrong.
Fire, fire I will shoot,
fire, fire I will shoot
so you will remember me,
terruco!
The young recruits as they pass
make the earth tremble
with their running feet.
Dust does not let you see
but you can hear
a sound without equal, ya!
They will be in the mountains,
the recruits will climb,
patrolling they will hunt
for the terruco with his FAL.
We will destroy where they live
and cut their throats.
To Castropampa you will go
and wherever you are
you will be a soldier.
Lily, lily, lily,
you are my downfall.
One hundred push-ups,
one hundred jumping jacks,
I am going to take it easy.

If they get me they will take me
let them take me, let them take me.
I am a sergeant, I am a recruit,
we are all tigers.
Only the monitor of my section
knows my suffering.
Leaping I go, climbing I go,
every morning.
In Ayacucho, Huanta, and Cangallo,
I do not know where I will land.
Better to stay in Huanta
and kill terrorists.

ONE DAY ON THE SHOOTING RANGE

The recruits were ready to practice shooting with rifles. At 4:30 that morning they were nervous. The monitors and military instructors called roll. Then the captain gave the order to march to the shooting range. The troop paraded through the front gate with their rifles under their arms. They were singing:

When my country was in danger,
I volunteered,
I proudly donned the green uniform
and said goodbye to my parents . . .

When we went through the streets of the city, people stood in their doorways to listen to the soldiers singing, maybe thinking their son was among them. The recruits did not rest or complain; they kept on singing:

Women, come out on your balconies,
the volunteers are passing by,
this morning their hearts are happy
with their military stripes.

The shooting range was far away. We had to walk a long distance. When we arrived, we found it full of brush, stones, and dirt that had been dug up. The older recruits, with a rank just above that of a soldier, spread out to take a look at the area, and others began to set

Rifle training with other new recruits at the shooting range. Photograph by Vicente, 1992.

up targets in the shape of human silhouettes at regulation distance from the line of shooters. Meanwhile, the monitors led our recruits in warming-up exercises.

"Roar!" "Yaaaa!" the troop answered weakly. Faced with that kind of response, the lieutenant became furious and ordered each of them to grab a handful of dirt and put it in his mouth. "Roar!" "Yaaaaaaaaa!" The Peruvian soldier's voice made nature shudder and birds fly, trying to find refuge behind the hills.

"Everyone ready?" "Ready!" they answered. "On your mark! In position! Ready or not! Fire!"

Of the ten bullets in the chamber, at least five had to hit the silhouette. If nine or ten hit their mark, you were classified as very good;

seven or eight, good; five or six, average; one, two or three, bad; and if you missed the target entirely, you were a notorious sluggard (*huevero*).[17]

The heat was unbearable that day, the gunpowder exuded the stench of war as wind whipped up the dust that impregnated our green uniforms. Over to one side, each recruit waited his turn.

Dusk fell on the shooting range. A few peasants who were passing by stopped to look in astonishment. After a while they went on their way, carrying their tools on their shoulders.

That day we stopped at six in the afternoon. An hour later the recruits had supper. Then they formed in front of their pavilions to sing, waiting for the bugle to call them to silence.

I lived in the military barracks for so many years. How many stories I would like to remember and tell. For example, I remember one whole night we stood at attention completely naked in the yard, because some uniforms had gone missing from the warehouse. I also think of the times we roamed the mountains hunting for Shining Path guerrillas.

We patrolled the areas of Razuhuillca, Macachacra, and the valleys around Huanta. On one occasion, in 1992 when we were headed in the direction of Chincho (in the region of Huancavelica), the guerrillas ambushed us. They killed the soldier who was standing guard. He had our communication radio. The bullet went through his chest and through the radio he was carrying on his back, and we couldn't make contact with the base at Huanta. Hungry and thirsty, we spent the whole afternoon lying on the ground. Every once in a while we raised a cap on a stick and it immediately received the impact of a bullet. After it got dark, we began to launch mortars and machine-gun fire. Later we returned to Huanta, carrying the dead soldier wrapped in a blanket. The following day, when the military went back with helicopters, they found the terrorists dead.

LAST YEARS IN THE ARMY

I returned to the base at Huanta in May 1993, after recuperating several months at the military hospital in Lima. Three months earlier I had been diagnosed with an internal hemorrhage.

When I arrived at the Huanta control post, hundreds of recruits were practicing marching back and forth to their monitors' orders. The base had changed its infrastructure, and its soldiers had also changed. Now the battalions of Cabitos were not only from Lima or Huaracha, but the so-called Ayacucho terrorists (*terrucos*), sons of the people, who had left that difficult clandestine life and enrolled in the Peruvian army, either voluntarily or because they were drafted.

As I walked to the commander's office to report my arrival, I heard some soldiers who knew me: "Good day, my sergeant!" I could feel the cold air from the snowy heights of Mount Razuhuillca on my face and hands. This was the coldest time of the year in the Peruvian Andes. Many people from the city and from the communities could be found lining up at the camp's medical facility. Only a few years before, the base had been off-limits to civilians.

The routine was the same, get up to the bugle call and go to sleep to the call for silence. Each day began with basic calisthenics, with or without arms. The songs we once sang as we ran through Huanta's streets had changed. No longer did we say: "Terrorist/if I find you/I will eat your head," but "Good day/the soldiers of Peru salute you."

The days went by in the usual routine: get up, bathe, exercise, go to the combat field, eat, and sleep. Sundays were our day off. That was good. Before, you were not allowed to go into town; they would have killed you by the time you got to the corner. But the young recruits always managed to escape to go to a fiesta or visit their girlfriends. When his obligatory military service was up, the reservist was taken by military plane to the city of Lima.

When I arrived from Lima that day, President Fujimori arrived in the afternoon aboard a helicopter. He descended with his colorful blanket on his shoulder. They said he had come to give Chinese cars to the communities.[18]

I had finished my middle school studies and I wanted to attend the Teachers Institute at Huanta. I hoped to get a degree in secondary education. The years had gone by very fast. When I went to pick up my belongings at the military warehouse (each time you left the base for a prolonged period of time they kept your things for you), I discovered my little green suitcase with the blue stripes, still doing its duty. It's true its colors had faded, and it had been repaired and then repaired again. I kept it because it was one of the things Lieutenant Shogun had given to me.

This was the same suitcase I used when, in 1987, I was taken to Los Cubitos barracks in Ayacucho, because a colonel was going to adopt me and I would be living at his house in Lima. I got there and they took me to the colonel's house. It was next to the offices of the Domingo Ayarza headquarters. I was there for something like three days. The colonel's wife, children, and a servant lived at that house. They made me sleep on the sofa. They asked me about my life and I told them. "You will be like part of our family. Tomorrow first thing we will travel to Lima," the lady said. They took us to the airport in a military car. I was sad but also happy. I was going to leave the barracks and enter a distant world. Who knew if I would return.

We waited for two or three hours, but there was no flight. The sky was overcast, and it rained but not hard. When they canceled the flight, we went back to the house. Because of some emergency, the colonel had been called to Lima in a military helicopter. They told me it would be better if I returned to the base at Huanta. I went with the next convoy. Later the colonel came back, but he was no longer interested in me.

After I retrieved my suitcase with the blue stripes, I went to the aid station. I stayed in Pavillion C. For the next few days I did guard duty at the control post, relieving the petty officers who normally had that job.

Before traveling to the military base at Viviana, I went out on patrol to Patasucro, near Huanta, and to the town of Churcampa in the region of Huancavelica.

We stayed in the peasant community of Patasucro for a month. The scant food we had brought with us didn't last. In the afternoon, in groups, we would go into the hills to hunt deer, or we'd trade for food.

We went from house to house, like at the beginning with Shining Path. On other days we looked for firewood and sweet *tumbo* fruits in the gorges (*huaycos*). And when we went to the town of Churcampa, we went out on patrol searching for terrorists in a totally inaccessible geographical area. We only heard their gunfire in the distance.

In August I was assigned to the base at Viviana. The convoys took

Skinning a deer we hunted near Viviana.

us as far as Cayarpachi. Then we walked six hours the rest of the way. I lived there for several months. We hunted crazy cattle that lived in the mountains and could be found near natural springs where they drink water.[19] We walked that whole vast geography that had been destroyed by Shining Path. There was little left. A group of terrorists had taken refuge in Chincho.

Sometimes we went on patrol with some religious sisters who were

On military patrol in Viviana, 1993.

missionaries from the Congregation of Jesus Verb and Victim.[20] They were on horseback. When we arrived in a peasant community they talked about God. They gave the peasants communion wafers that had been consecrated by a priest who came to Viviana now and then from the city of Huancavelica.

Once, when we were climbing from Chincho to Viviana, the mother sister spoke to me in the following way: "You could be a priest!" I responded with an innocent laugh, and said: "No, Mother, I have grave sins. Surely God would kick me out." "No, no!" she said, "God came into this world looking for sinners." The mother's words caused me to dream that I was wearing sackcloth, curing bullet wounds, giving water to the thirsty, and mediating between the members of Shining Path and the soldiers.

But, more than a dream, this seemed like the opportunity I had been waiting for since childhood. To be able to do something for those who had nothing, for my countrymen we had so brutally mistreated, stealing from them and raping their women. And so I began to think this was the institution I was looking for, and that I would try to find a way to become a member.

One day I told my immediate superior at the Viviana base: "I am leaving," just like back in 1983 when I told my aunt: "I am leaving." The lieutenant said: "Think about it for a while. You will die of hunger, and it will not be long now before you achieve the rank of petty officer." But I had made up my mind to abandon the army, the home where I grew up and learned to read and write. Once again I would be homeless. I would go and live like the lilies and birds in the countryside, but now instead of the red-and-white flag it would be the white one that would accompany me for a while.

In Santa Rosa de Ocopa. On my way to the school to teach the children catechism.
Photograph by Miguel, 1997.

TIME IN THE FRANCISCAN CONVENT 3

I was the bell-ringer.[1]

I set the alarm clock on my bedside table so I would be sure to wake up on time. This was yet another sort of life: the struggle for egalitarian communism through peaceful means. Miguel James, my *compañero* when we joined the Franciscan family, reminded me of the following day's activities: "Don't forget, your job is to ring the bell." He and I slept in the same room. Ringing that bell was a daily activity. Upon hearing its sudden sound, all we postulants (what they call those who have just entered the convent) got out of bed and went to breakfast. They also rang the bell to call us to lunch, dinner, and the various liturgical activities. The only time they did not ring that first bell of the day was when it was somebody's birthday. They wanted to be able to surprise that person with a serenade while he slept. Each night as I lay on my cot, before doing my life review, I would think about the following day.[2] And I thought about myself and my family of origin. Many months had passed since I'd joined the Franciscan family.

Before getting into the car at the Viviana military base, and saying my definitive goodbye to the army, I had told the Jesus Verb and Victim missionary mother: "I am going in search of God." She gave me her blessing and a letter of introduction to the Magdalena parish in Ayacucho. A few days later I arrived at Cipriani's Ayacucho home.[3] The man was seated, wearing his cassock of purple stripes, his skull-cap on his head,[4] a large cross on his chest, and a ring on his finger. He did not offer me his hand. He said only: "Sit there." Then he said: "Tell me about your life."

I began by telling him I had been in the army, but the moment I said that his attitude changed. He became very serious, even accusatory: "Is it not true that prostitutes visit the barracks?" When I said it is true, he said: "You cannot be a priest, son." I asked myself: if I had told him I had been in the Peruvian Communist Party, what would the cleric have said? He might have fainted. Good God, a sinner as a candidate to the priesthood! After a brief silence, he told me to leave: "Go back home and pray to God." I left his house almost in tears. It was next to the Paola Church near Ayacucho's Central Park. I returned to Huanta. There I worked for a while hauling rocks and collecting the fleshy pads of prickly pears used to make fertilizer.

Once, after a day carrying rocks, I again ran into the mother of Jesus Verb and Victim. I told her about my meeting with Cipriani, and she said: "Let us knock on another door." She introduced me to the Franciscan Mothers of Huanta. They gave me some pamphlets about convocations to select Franciscan candidates. A few months later, I attended one of those convocations.

In January 1995, we went through the stage of aspirant (aspirante), that is to say, the process of selecting candidates. We all wanted to be Franciscans but, as Jesus said: "Many are called but few are chosen." And so we chosen ones were few. That part of the process lasted a month. We took psychological exams and academic tests. And we had personal interviews. We also saw films about the saints. In the lectures they told us: "This is a hard life. Many say I want to be a Franciscan but later quit."

In order to take the vow of chastity, it is necessary for you to have had a sexual experience with a woman. Some said: "Yes, I have had girlfriends," others said they had not. Every evening we would sing along with our teacher. One of the songs that stayed with me is "Francis, Living Evangelist":

I was a troubadour, they called me Francis.
I sang happily in the nights of Assisi,
but I do not want to sing of Rolando,
nor of the exploits of Amadis.
In my heart I felt total emptiness
and discovered a different path.
I do not want loves that pass and die,
today I sing only to my immortal King.
I want to be a living evangelist
and abandon myself in your arms, Lord.

The candidate period ended. The teacher priest informed us that only seven of the forty who had applied would enter the convent. We were nervous. They told me I had been accepted.

A month later, on March 16, 1995 — my birthday — and accompanied by the priest who was the postulants' teacher, I entered the convent vestibule to experience the fascinating world of religious life.[5] How exciting it was for some, what a disappointment for others! I walked slowly through those broad and silent halls, the colonial cloisters where great columns met in arches. The ceilings were made of wood. I passed walls made of mud and straw, where valuable colonial paintings hung: it all spoke to me of spiritual life, study, and meditation.

Some of the brothers walked those halls, talking among themselves or reciting the rosary. We went through three cloisters before we came to the postulants' hall. The young second-year postulants looked out and welcomed me. Then the priest showed me to my room. That convent had been founded as a receiving home in 1595 by Friar Andrés Corso. Saint Francis Solano was its first provincial minister. It is the main parish of Lima province. Juan Landázuri Ricketts also lived there.[6]

Those of us who had been selected as postulants where formally admitted in a special ceremony. To applause, we four "brothers" presented ourselves at the ritual Mass, where they gave us our Franciscan cross (tau).[7] The Mass was held at Lima's Temple of the Barefoot Brothers.

My "father" teacher was like an officer in the army. At five in the morning he got us up to do exercises. Not spiritual exercises, but those that would strengthen our legs so we would be able to undertake the Franciscan missions. Before it was light, we ran around the cloister for fifteen minutes. The brothers were still asleep. Then, as the sun cast its first rays behind Mount San Cristóbal, we did calisthenics such as push-ups, pull-ups, knee bends, and jumping jacks. Half an hour later we took showers, and then, in different parts of the cloister, read the Bible out loud. After that we heard Mass.

We had to eat breakfast in military style: quickly. At eight it was time to go to class: high school for those who had just arrived, and those in their second year attended Lima's School of Pontifical and Civil Theology. At one we were back at the convent. In the afternoon we received classes in urbanity, liturgy, the Bible, and ethics. On Saturday, during morning prayer, we sang "Salve Regina" in Latin, led by Father Oña:

> Salve, Regina, mater misericordae: vita dulce do, et pes nostra
> salve.
> Ad te clamamus, exsules, filii hebae.
> As te suspiramus, gementes, et flentes in hac lagrimaum valle.
> Eia ergo, advocate nostra, illos tuos miericordes oculos ad nos
> converte.
> Et Jesum, benedictum fructum ventris tui,
> Nobis post hoc exsilium ostende.
> O Clemens: o pia: o dulcis Virgo María.

That day I got up at 4:30 in the morning. I did not ring the bell, as was our custom on a day when there was a birthday. Instead, I went from room to room, waking my *compañeros*. A few minutes later, we were serenading our brother who celebrated his special day:

> Lord, today we thank you
> for life, earth, and sun.
> Lord, today we want to sing
> the glory of your gifts.

There were no exercises that day. For this reason we always loved birthdays. In the afternoon, the vicar in charge bought candies, chocolates, sandwiches (*chisitos*), a cake, champagne, and sodas. The party began after dinner. In the old dining room we danced to popular music; and we ate and drank. We really enjoyed those occasions.

THE FRANCISCAN BROTHERS

I knew a lot of saintly Franciscan brothers, who devoted their lives to the poor. What does it mean to be saintly? It means transcending the human condition. On the other hand, most of the brothers—from the time of our novitiate we were all called brothers—had our defects like any other human being. Those stereotypes believed by the faithful— that we were all angels, that our hands could work miracles—are not true. History accepts those ideas even less. We were simply good men helping our community.

In our period as postulants, my friend Cachón—the nickname we gave Josué—arrived with candies in his backpack for us all. He thought that, as Franciscans, we should walk barefooted, love the poor and those who were our enemies, and not look at pretty women. For him, the Bible was God's divine word dictated to Moses on Mount Sinai.

During the novitiate we were able to open our eyes and see—as Plato taught—that behind the red and yellow flowers there was another flower: the true one, finer and more pure because what we see are only copies. And that is how the Bible is; Adam and Eve weren't real people, there was no flood, Abraham was not how he was described. Those were only metaphors used to explain other things that were more important. And finally, not even God existed in human form. Our teacher explained that if God looked like his pictures he would not be God. God did not have a beard; we only imagined him that way. God exists in time and space. He is good and bad. He is our neighbor.[8]

In order to live the religious life in the manner of Saint Francis, two things were necessary: vocation and perseverance.

We tied our habit at the waist with a white rope. This rope had three knots, symbolizing our vows: chastity, obedience, and poverty. Chastity was one of the requisites for being a brother. You had to forget about sexual relations, you couldn't even think about them. The truth is, Franciscan missionary brothers do not live hidden away in a convent like their brothers who are cloistered. We lived in community with the people. When we attended classes at the Franciscan Center, where all Lima's Franciscans—sisters and brothers—came together, we might fall in love. Or, when we went out to teach catechism to young students, and came in contact with beautiful girls, one or another brother might be smitten. But then the lessons in Franciscan spirituality made us forget those objects of our affection, because we learned they were our brothers and sisters in Christ's blood.

When I was at the novitiate convent at Ocopa, many people came to the August fiesta of Santa Rosa de Ocopa. We novices, dressed in our sackcloth, served as guides, taking them around the premises. To those visitors we were like angels. We showed them the chapel, the art gallery with its canvases, the museum, the library with its valuable books, and we rang the bell that, according to the priest, bid us obey whatever it asked of us. But the hardest part was answering the visitors' questions. They wanted us to show them the tunnel we used to visit the sisters, or how we resisted the temptation of women.

At the Juan Landázuri Rickets Institute of Philosophy we discussed priestly marriage with the professors. Priests could marry because they lived alone. The argument for not having a wife was that Jesus did not have one. Priests studied for six or seven years; then they were ordained and assigned a parish. There they lived from the money they collected by offering masses for the departed, and officiating at marriages, baptisms, and such. But we brothers lived in community; marriage was not possible for us. Furthermore, now and then we rotated from convent to convent, like soldiers or members of Shining Path.

The next knot on our rope symbolized obedience. This was an important vow. Just as in the army, you had to obey unquestioningly, in silence. We all had a hard time with that one.

The last knot stood for poverty. You might ask: what poverty? But we had to understand poverty differently. Following in Jesus's footsteps, you observe the vow of poverty in its spiritual and social dimensions. You live like the "lesser ones" of today,[9] without falling prey to egoism and consumerism, rejecting those temptations that drag men into misery.

We had our cars, our access to the Internet. We had good cooks, balanced meals with wine and sometimes beer. We had servants who washed our clothes. We attended expensive private schools. We also took trips to different parts of the country, and some students traveled abroad.

There are excellent brothers at the Franciscan monasteries: humble, unconditionally ministering to the needy. The father who lives at Puerto Ocopa Mission is like that. Thanks to such men, I learned the virtues of tolerance and solidarity. With other priests, you might leave Mass disgusted by the sermon. Others even threw things at the cook. All kinds of men were there. This is why we say that God reflects the good and the bad.

In this context, for example, we had a priest who was always drunk. He loved to drink. He was always reading the paper looking for wedding parties, and he would show up. When he died, run over by a car in the streets of Lima, we found bottles of Cartavio rum in this room.

Another brother suffered from amnesia. He forgot everything. Every little while he would eat a meal, because he forgot he had eaten earlier.

Cardenal Juan Landázuri, before he was named bishop of Lima, had been the provincial general of the Missionary Province of Saint Francis Solano of Peru. On his birthday, every December 19, he would come to the convent of the barefoot brothers to celebrate. On that day our cooks prepared a special meal, like roast turkey with applesauce. After dinner in the refectory, we would converse with our cardinal. On January 16, 1997, before I became a novice, they brought his body to the convent in a casket. The brothers intoned the hymn of farewell:

At the dusk of life
they tested my love
asking if I offered a cup of water to the thirsty.

We wept at his death. And so, some fathers died but others took their place. "We will die, and you will continue to spread the Gospel," the fathers said. The priest who taught us our class in urbanity and was also the minister general, died one morning while celebrating Mass. We ran to help him, but he was already gone.

NOVITIATE AT OCOPA
A clean blue sky spread above the Mantaro Valley. We were on our way to Jauja. Immense green fields stretched before our eyes. Between the

trees we could see the Mantaro River, softly murmuring but polluted by the Oroya mine. We could not yet see the town of Ocopa, but for hours we had felt relief from Lima's heat. Now, coming through the window, a cool breeze refreshed our temples. The fields planted with corn, artichokes, and peas swayed in the gentle winds of March.

Our bus passed along a road bordered by pine and eucalyptus trees, welcoming the traveler. We peered out the window, trying to get a look at our new home, the convent of Santa Rosa de Ocopa.

I spent a wonderful year at that marvelous convent. I learned a lot from its silence and hospitality. And this was where I donned the Franciscan habit on March 16, 1998.

Father Francisco of San José founded the convent of Santa Rosa de Ocopa in 1725. In 1758 it was elevated to the category of Apostolic College of the Doctrine of the Faith. From then on, the Jauja valley was Christianized by Franciscan and Dominican missionaries. They established many different convents. The convent of Ocopa was closed in 1824 due to a decree issued by Simón Bolívar. The community ceased to exist, and all the missions were lost. It was restored in 1836. A number of Peruvian convents were reestablished at that time. Raúl Porras Barrenechea called the place "Ocopa, perennial center of Peruvian life and evangelical light."[10]

Today the convent is made of up four colonial-style cloisters. It stands beside the original convent, which is just as its founder built it. They call it the Obrería. Thick columns sustain galleries of broad corridors constructed around inner patios. In 1955 it was declared a National Monument. It is famous for its library of twenty thousand volumes, many of them works of great historic and bibliographic value. They are written in Latin and Spanish, and date from the sixteenth, seventeenth, and eighteenth centuries. This library doesn't only have books on religion and theology, but also works of history, geography, philosophy, natural sciences, medicine, literature, and linguistics.

CEREMONY UPON ENTERING THE NOVITIATE

We formally entered the novitiate on March 16, 1997. The Christian population received us in the temple singing: "They come in joy, Lord, singing they come in joy." After the words of greeting by the priest who celebrated the Mass, and before the act of penance, we became novices.

Each of us was called by name. In loud clear voices we answered: "Present!" Then we lined up facing the priest. The provincial said: "Dear brothers, what do you ask of our fraternity? In unison, we responded: "Compelled by God's mercy, teach us to follow the poor and crucified Christ, to live in poverty, obedience, and chastity. Teach us, as well, to be faithful in prayer, to live our penance in continual conversion, to serve the Church and all men, to be of one heart and one soul with all of you. Teach us at every moment the demands of spreading Christ's Gospel, following the rules of evangelical life, and observing the law of fraternal love that He and our father Saint Francis bequeathed us."

Then the provincial said: "May all-merciful God keep you in His grace, and may Jesus Christ Himself illuminate, accompany and strengthen you." Everyone in the church said: "Amen." As the Mass continued, each of us novices was given a Bible and the symbol of the Franciscan cross. They blessed us. The next day we would officially begin our religious formation as Franciscan brothers.

We began each day in the chapel, celebrating the Eucharist. Then we went to the church to play the harmonium at Masses for the departed or for birthdays, depending on what was on the agenda when each of us took his turn. Classes began at eight in the morning: history of the Franciscan order, catechism, Bible, Latin, music, and liturgy. Before lunch we had midday prayers, and while we ate we listened to a novice read about Franciscan spirituality. Classes resumed again after our afternoon siesta. At six in the evening we had vespers, followed by dinner. Then we had recreation, hours during which we could relax or play. Our day ended with prayers in the chapel. This was the novice's life.

Throughout our novitiate year, we had monthly life reviews, similar to what we had in the Peruvian Communist Party. The difference was that here we had to forgive ourselves not seven times over as Christ did, but seventy times seven, which is to say continuously. Forgiveness was a constant in our lives, while in the party threats and executions had been the constants. At our life reviews the secretary took notes on everything we said, in order to pass them on to the priest who was our teacher. In most of our life reviews we would argue about one thing or another.

We studied Franciscan spirituality, analysis of the Bible, Latin, Franciscan history, mission history, and music. Our classes ran from Monday through Thursday, because on Fridays we would visit area schools in order to prepare the students to receive their first communion.[11]

SUNDAY OUTING

After a week of study, Sundays were free. We would leave the convent and go to Miraflores or some of the slum towns (*pueblos jóvenes*).[12] We always went out in a group, never alone. We went out alone only when we reached the student brother stage.[13] During the novitiate we were not supposed to get to know the cities, but go into the highlands and gorges. We wore sandals and loose-fitting clothing. We hiked up mountains where we often saw deer. In the gorges we found wild fruits ripening on the trees, and we would pick and eat them.

Some Sundays we used ropes to climb off steep precipices. We took serious risks. One Sunday we decided to go in another direction. Instead of the mountains, we went to a river near the city, to fish for trout. Almost at the end of our novitiate, we visited the lagoon near Sierra Lumi and the Satipo highway, where Andrés A. Cáceres ambushed a group of Chilean soldiers.[14] Our *compañero* Paddy took off all his clothes and dived into the lagoon's cold water. The local people stared at us. We told Paddy: "Put your shorts on."

HOURS IN THE NOVITIATE CELL

A multitude of thoughts filled my head when I sat long hours immersed in the silence of my cell. There I was able to engage with long-relegated memory. Without anyone to whom I could tell my experiences, I had kept them to myself. I remembered that when I was studying at Lima's School of Pontifical and Civil Theology, a philosophy professor had asked: "Why don't you write about your life?" She said: "It is interesting."[15] That is when I began to write in a notebook. I know that life has taught me a great deal every day, but much of what it taught also left me with questions.

There are moments I will never forget, like during my adolescence when I was a comrade or young recruit, and with a mother's tenderness the military and then the Franciscans took me in. And so life filled me with the desire to live and tell some of my stories, like when I walked with a rifle or red flag on my shoulder, or when I was in the convent and—wearing Franciscan sackcloth—read the Bible and wrote. Sometimes I would take my guitar and go to see Mario, one of my fellow novices. He taught me how to tune the instrument, and how to sing. This is one of his compositions:

Lord, I ask you to touch this blind man.
Today I am a man who wants to see
all your wonders.
I know it is easier with your light,
I know I can see with your light.

Soon we would hear the bell telling us to go to the chapel to commence midday prayers (Sexta) and then to lunch.[16]

Every day, as we ate one of us would pray out loud, both at lunch and dinner. The themes were Franciscan spirituality, from the book *Little Flowers of Saint Francis*. Before it was our turn to read, we had to practice. The father would interrupt us to point out our errors. How many times did they correct the way I read? Very often. Always. It is painful to humbly accept those criticisms in public. When the Franciscan brothers finished their meal, the reader could begin to eat.

CONFESSING TO THE PRIEST IN THE NOVITIATE

In our novitiate classes they taught us the importance of the sacrament of confession. Jesus Christ gave this power to Peter, the first pope, telling him: "What was settled on earth will be settled in heaven, and that which was rent asunder on earth will be rent asunder in heaven." Confession was secret; if the priest divulged something told to him in confession it was a grave sin. And so, once outside the confessional, priests forgot everything they heard.

During the novitiate we confessed once a month to the priest in the chapel where we celebrated the Eucharist and divine office. We knelt before the father, who looked straight into our repentant eyes, and awaited his response. We had to reveal all that we had done wrong, and all our impure acts or, as our teacher said, "all the *miskis*," lustful thoughts we might have had. The priest told me I should pray twenty Our Fathers and many Ave Marías in penance. It was embarrassing to tell everything we had done wrong, but if you confessed without lying you left feeling lighter. If you did not, you were uncomfortable and little by little would lie again.

OUR MISSIONARY EXPERIENCE IN THE FOREST: JOURNEY TO SATIPO MISSION

Around five in the afternoon, on November 27, 1997, four novices from Ocopa—Brother Paddy, Brother Mario, Brother Miguel, and Brother Lurgio—accompanied and supervised by our good Brother Roque, set out for the mission at Satipo.[17] As the car advanced, we left behind the Ocopa sanctuary. Soon dusk fell, casting its delicate shadows over the Mantaro Valley. In the dark, all we could see was the illuminated cross on Mount Jerusalem, placed there by Father Carlos Lafuente.

Passing Jauja, we began to climb. The landscape changed. It was cold. Now we were at Lomo Largo. Before we arrived in Tarma, we descended again, feeling the heat of the mountain once more. As it got warmer, we passengers took off our jackets. At Satipo you can wear light clothing. It is hotter in Puerto Ocopa, but even in the most intense heat Franciscan missionaries cannot remove their saintly habits.

Around three in the morning we arrived at the town of Satipo. We had been traveling for nine hours. For what seemed like a long time we slept on benches in the park. But finally the new day broke through, with its tenuous light. Forest birds began flying through the branches of the trees. With our sleepy eyes, we looked around us, in every direction. When we arrived at the Satipo mission we ate our breakfast enthusiastically, animated by the brilliant anecdotes of some Franciscan missionaries from Atalaya who were also there.

VISITING THE DIFFERENT FRANCISCAN MISSION HOUSES: PICHANAKI MISSION

When we had finished breakfast around eight in the morning, the hour when the sun begins to shine on Satipo as the city fills with the sounds of merchants, travelers, and motorcycle taxis moving about, we set out for the station where the buses leave for Pichanaki. After a couple of hours on the road, we arrived at Pichanaki Mission. Father Brother Felipe welcomed us. After greeting us all, he invited us to see the house.

"Man is only worth what he does," as the Franciscan saying goes. Through his example of charity and hard work, Brother Felipe played an important evangelizing role.

We saw all the mission's areas: pastoral hall, catechism room, and garden. Finally we entered the church, which was in the process of reconstruction. "During the worst of the terrorist era, we had some difficult moments," the priest said, showing us a series of bullet holes in the church's wall. The machine-gun fire had ravaged one side of the tabernacle and had gone through the altar and the acolyte's chair. The priest and his faithful had been caught in the middle of Mass.

But in spite of everything, they had been able to double their missionary work, preaching life and peace in the midst of violence. Now, little by little, they were rebuilding the church.

AT PUERTO OCOPA MISSION

That same November, on the twenty-ninth, we took a van (combi) to the mission at Puerto Ocopa.[18] Our vehicle traveled for some time over a road of reddish yellow earth. We passed fields of pineapple, papaya, and oranges. A river ran along one side of the road.

When we arrived at the Puerto Ocopa Mission, we were welcomed by Father Brother Teodorico Castillo, the war-orphaned children (asháninkas) who lived there, and some Franciscan mothers of the Fraternity of the Immaculate Conception, religious sisters devoted to caring for and educating orphan children.

The landscape is beautiful. Two rivers meet here. The Pampa Hermosa-Satipo descends from the heights of Toctuga Lagoon, where Brother Francisco Irazola's highway twists and turns before it reaches Puerto Ocopa. Then it joins with the Mazamari and they become the Pangoa, whose waters sing among the stones and seem to hurry as they join the Perené, which, together with the Tambo, holds memories of a number of Ocopa's martyrs.[19]

The house at Puerto Ocopa is surrounded by fruit trees, avocado, mango, lemon, star fruit, and coconut. Animals graze in the orchard.

Father Teodorico came to Puerto Ocopa in 1957, replacing Brother

Antonio Rojas. From the moment he arrived, he was just another brother of the people. Like the Apostle Paul: "I made myself a Jew to the Jews" (1 Corinthians 9:20). The aging missionary wore dark gray sackcloth, a straw hat, and rubber sandals. When someone asked him something, he remained silent for a moment and then responded with care. In the afternoons he walked with his short steps as he prayed the office of the day. His voice became one with nature, producing a monotonous music of praise.

Looking with admiration at the priest, you might wonder if he understood a missionary's work. Maybe, like some primitive landscape, he had become distant and insensitive. "It can be depressing at times," he said, "but it is important to pick yourself up and try harder." The missionary's radical, unconditional option spoke louder than words.

It was around seven at night when Father Castillo blessed the food we were about to eat. Sitting around the table, we engaged in enthusiastic conversation while, outside in the patio, the children ran and played and sang.

Soon we were installed in the dormitory. Heat seeped in through the roof, but the river sang softly, inviting us to sleep.

The next day, the first Sunday of Advent in Christian liturgy,[20] began like any other with the sound of birds in the forest. It was a symphony. The morning sun began to bring the trees to life, while a light mist rose, leaving crystalline dewdrops on the green grass. We celebrated Sunday Mass with the songs of the orphans (asháninkas) who made their home at the mission. The Franciscan father had taken these children in. Their fathers and mothers were killed during the violence.

On Monday afternoon we bathed in the river one last time. In order to cross the Pangoa, we walked along its bank, calculating the distance to the opposite side. We jumped in and began to swim. The cool water was a joy, but we had to keep our eyes open for whirlpools and current. We had to stay calm. Soon we found ourselves on the other shore.

On Tuesday morning we returned to Satipo in order to say goodbye to the family at Puerto Ocopa. Soon the road and mountains were only memories. As the vehicle moved on, we left it all behind.

AT SATIPO MISSION

Father Brother Mario Brown's missionary work at Satipo is arduous and admirable. He cares for more than forty people a month. He celebrates Mass, baptizes, and catechizes. In fact, he is the missionary who attends to all the nearby towns. I am sure that as he walks he says, like the Apostle Paul: "I should be punished if I did not preach the gospel" (First Corinthians 9:16), and "I still do this, for the sake of the gospel" (First Corinthians 9:23).

Very early each day, with his bag hanging from his shoulder, Father Mario goes out to the different communities accompanied by a catechist by the name of Nemesio. I do not know how Nemesio and Andrés discovered their catechist vocations. Maybe they ran into the missionary on the road and asked him: "Missionary, where are you going so happily? Why do you sing all the time? What nostalgias nest in your soul? I would like to share your ideal" (a Franciscan song).

We experienced missionary work on two occasions. Early one morning we set out for Santa Bibiana. The car left us in Santa Rosita, and from there we continued on foot along the Satipo River. It kept raining, and a thick mist prevented us from seeing the forest landscape.

In Santa Bibiana four children made their first communion. Two were orphans (ashâninkas) and the other two peasants from the mountains who had come to live in this zone. At the celebration of the Eucharist we saw the faces of men, women, and children who took part in the different songs with great animation and concentration. In his homily, the priest, besides encouraging and nourishing their faith, told them: "It would be a good thing for you to have a party, for it is an opportune time for you to get to know each other better, so you can share your faith in work, sorrow, and joy. The faith of each of us is like a candle that lights itself: maybe a busybody comes along and blows one out, but he can never blow out a hundred candles all burning together."

In the silence of the afternoon, when you can hear the murmur of the universe, the sun fell slowly below the horizon. This was our last day at Satipo Mission.

We had fulfilled our curiosity to learn about the missions. Now all we had to do was persevere and nurture our desire to "mature" in Christ's teachings.

Throughout the day we walked with Brother Miguel James, admissions master in the Francisco order, and talked on the balcony of the mission house as we looked out at the garden planted with native trees: avocados, mangos, and coconuts. The fragrance of wildflowers filled the air.

RETURN TO SANTA ROSA DE OCOPA

On Friday, around eight in the morning, we boarded the vehicle that would take us back to Santa Rosa de Ocopa.

Once again, we followed the missionaries' footsteps. The marvelous landscape stretched before us, filled with hanging waterfalls with their clear waters. "Along the way we may see deer, peccaries, and armadillos," our driver said. But none were to be seen.

As the day progressed, we left behind the towns of Santa Rosita, San Dionisio, Santa Bibiana, Santa Ana, Mariposa, San Antonio, Apalla, Calabaza, Toldopampa, Sierra Lumi, Comas, and Pumaqucha Lagoon. As we descended into the Mantaro Valley, the sun died on the horizon. Our car moved more slowly because there were men working on the highway. And then dusk fell, covering everything with its mysterious shadows. We stopped looking out the window and let our heads fall back. When we rounded the last curve coming into the town of Santa Rosa de Ocopa, the clock in the church tower paused between each of seven hammer strokes against its bell.

DONNING FRANCISCAN ROBES

It started out cloudy that day. At six in the morning the bells began to ring at the Ocopa sanctuary. We were ready to profess our vows and become student brothers, the next stage in our journey. When we entered the church from the sacristy, it was full of faithful. Incense floated up into the cupola, a profusion of flowers were on the altar, and the Franciscan fathers were at the back, dressed in white:[21] The choir sang:

> Missionary, where are you going so joyously?
> Why are you always singing?
> What nostalgias nest in your soul?
> I want to share your ideal. (Repeat.)

As with Christ and Francisco,
the greatest thing is love!
Like Christ and Francisco,
I want to be a missionary!
Because I search for a life of meaning,
my desire is to live the Gospel,
to give my life for my brothers.
Like Christ, love until death. (Repeat.)

When they called us up we approached the altar, and the two of us who were going to consecrate ourselves stood before the celebrant. Then the provincial said: "Dear brothers, what do you ask of God, the Holy Church, and our Franciscan order?" We answered: "Called by the goodness of God, after having lived in Franciscan fraternity during the years of our novitiate, we ask to be admitted to the life of lesser brothers, with the promise of observing, for one year, the evangelical teachings of obedience, poverty, and chastity."

At the end we all said: "We give thanks to God." Then, standing, the celebrant said: "Lord, in your grace listen to the prayers of your people." Immediately he sat down. Two Franciscan fathers served as our witnesses. Each of us approached the celebrant and knelt.

"Dear brother: before our Lord who has called and convoked us to the Church, to the community of God to which we belong, and before the Franciscan family, do you declare your willingness to consecrate yourself to the Lord in religious life?" We answered: "Provincial Brother I, moved by divine inspiration, wish to consecrate myself to follow closely in the footprints of Jesus Christ and to faithfully observe the Gospel in your hands. I pledge myself to God almighty, to live for a year in obedience, without egotism, and in chastity; I promise always to follow the life and rules established by Pope Honorio, in line with the general constitutions of the order of lesser brothers. In this way, I give myself wholeheartedly to this fraternity." Then the celebrant said: "And I, as a representative of almighty God, promise that if you faithfully obey you will have eternal life. In the name of the Father, the Son, and the Holy Ghost."

The rite of first profession to enter this next stage ended when the celebrant gave us the Bible and the Rules of Saint Francis.

THE FRANCISCAN CENTER OF PERU

On March 30, 1998, the Franciscan Philosophical Theological Institute was inaugurated, fulfilling a Franciscan brother's dream. On a cool afternoon we gathered in one of the halls of the Franciscan Center of Peru. It was December 17, 1998, and we had just finished our first academic year with a fraternal reunion of professors and students.

Almost all the professors were there and we, the fifteen brothers who had studied in the four departments: Twelve Apostles, Saint Francis Solano, Saint Joseph of the Amazon, and Holy Name of Jesus.

The head of the Institute, Father Gustavo, welcomed us all. As is usual at Franciscan gatherings, he made his speech with a glass of champagne in his hand: "Welcome, brothers, to this gathering. We want to share a moment at the end of this academic year. We want to retrieve and preserve the philosophy and theology of the Franciscan school. We have no reason to envy the Peruvian universities in any way, because here we study the same disciplines." He ended with a toast of appreciation and good wishes for Christmas and the New Year of 1999.

Although I had found the necessary peace and tranquility in the convent, and although I had finally had the time I needed to reflect upon my life, I began to feel that this was probably not the place for me. Something deep within told me I would soon be leaving.

This small room invited study and the search for peace, quiet, and a feeling of oneness with nature. The barefoot brothers' monastery was surrounded by green gardens, colorful flowers, and healing silence. We had lived a year of rich experiences. We had learned a great deal. I will always remember my first Latin class, when the professor said: "Here we must resuscitate Latin." For this and for so many other gifts, it was necessary for me to thank God for the moments He had given me.

Then, in an atmosphere of friendship, in Franciscan style, we enjoyed chocolate with *panettone*. The enthusiasm and joy were contagious. We could not forget the songs that characterize the Franciscans. Accompanied by the strumming of guitars we sang "The Living Gospel," "Good Father" and others. Then, we danced to a medley of

Andean songs (huaynos).[22] The guitars passed from hand to hand. Each brother sang a song from the place he had come from: Arequipa, Huancabamba, Huanta, Juliaca, Tebas, Lima. Each brother has his own character: one is quiet, another sings, and sometimes fifteen brothers in unison sing and dance to the rhythm of the huayno.

If we asked our brother aspirants, postulants, novices, and teachers why they chose this lifestyle, I am sure each of them would tell a different story. This is mine, not so different from those of many of my countrymen. Maybe I was a little more fortunate to have lived within these institutions. But most important during my stage of religious life was having come in contact with the works of men such as Jesus and Saint Francis of Assisi, who not only preached but practiced what they preached. They exalted the importance of being human. They elevated the dignity of man in the hope of erasing borders and eliminating racism.

Later, Brother Juan passed Christmas cards out to the professors, congratulating them on behalf of the Institute's students. Brother Milton thanked the provincial ministers and mentors who had made the Institute run so smoothly. He also acknowledged the patience and dedication of the professors.

At the end of the evening we finished singing to the Lord, who had brought water and the Spirit to life yet again. And once more, Father Gustavo thanked us all.

After that first academic year at the Juan Landázuri Ricketts Philosophical and Theological Institute, I took a vacation. Upon my return from that brief change of scene, I left religious life.

That vacation had given me the opportunity to think about my life. I looked back upon it and could no longer imagine myself in the convent. I wanted to have a family, maybe even a child, and to live in the world like any ordinary person.

My plan was to return to my village, to the quiet life of a farmer. But the future held more surprises. A few months later I would have the opportunity to enter the university. Without even knowing exactly what it was, I decided to study anthropology. In a short time I was convinced that this could be my vocation.

I RETURN TO THE COUNTRYSIDE OF AYACUCHO 4

I always wanted to return to the places where I once walked, my head filled with such utopian thoughts about how the country might change: that idle land of Alan García's farm dog.[1] But what do those distant lands—strange, forgotten by the owner class—possess that beckons one back? There, where indigenous peoples killed one another, where my brother and my friends all died? Can I say we did not suffer on that land back then? Can I say we were not hungry? Maybe the César Miró waltz is right: "Everyone Returns" to the place where he was born and grew up.[2] Or maybe I just wanted to retrace the pathways where I walked, like the Andean soul that retraces all roads taken before life ends, in order to die in peace.[3] Or maybe, finally, as a human being it is simply about dust returning to dust. Twenty years had passed and I went back to look for myself along the trail.[4]

Before that painful return, I donned the clothes I had worn the day before, and the week before that: dark blue jeans, the same clothes I had worn for years, well used by time. I had some money saved and thought about buying something decent, maybe something I could also wear at my job as a university professor, so people would not always see me in the same old thing. But no, that morning I went out instead and bought a small bottle of liquor, some cigarettes, bread,

OPPOSITE: I walk toward the peasant communities of Ayacucho. Photograph by Isabel García, 2007.

and a few cans of tuna. I felt like I was going to meet friends in those places, or that my *compañeros* from the war might still be there.

On Saturday, September 29, 2007, I left the city of Ayacucho around five in the morning. Climate and ecology changed as the bus advanced, as it climbed or descended Peru's deep river geography. We passed through hot Muyurina Valley, Chacco, and Pacaycasa where farmers combine working the land with the manufacture of perfect bricks. The peasants had not yet gone out into their fields. Their homes had smoke rising from the chimneys. Hardworking women must already have been preparing the day's food, to beat the sun that had begun to paint the eastern sky.

Later we crossed the Wari Bridge. The Waris were the first Peruvians to urbanize; they worked stone and preserved their dead. The cold zone begins farther up, around the community of Quinua where artisans draw with earth and display their rich culture. Near the community of Quinua are the lands of Mounts Quinua and Condorcunca, where in 1824 Spaniards and Peruvians fought the battle of Ayacucho. From then on, bloodshed has been a constant, feeding the people's deep familiarity with death. Or maybe, with its series of rebellions, the spilling of blood dates to even more remote times. Higher up is Apacheta, the mountain considered to be the protector of all peasant communities and of truckers. That is where the Andean animals graze: llamas and alpacas, cows and sheep. That is where the deer (*viscachas*) and eagles live.

Along the way, people have built their cemeteries. Christian crosses can be seen here and there. Burial sites bearing symbols of automobile accidents, or dating to the times of violence: the graves of those assassinated by the military, village militia, or Shining Path.

The passengers begin reading from the book of memory. This is where my brother died! My uncle died here! Right here is where the car turned over! From time to time one can see the helper who collects the bus fares jump off to place sprigs of flowers for Lord Wamani among the dark rocks.[5] Or one observes the drama of suffering of those who communicate with their beloved dead by lighting candles and offering up their aroma and the colors of the flowers. And there is no lack of highway police waiting to receive their 2 soles bribe. Then the road descends again, toward the city of Tambo.

The cold air glancing off the window cooled my temples and I, who had come hoping to see what I had not been able to see before, began matching the vehicle's rhythm with all those circumstances I had lived. I closed my eyes and was overwhelmed by memories of love. Before I left Ayacucho, I called Isabel. She and I spent a lot of time together. She saw me, listened to me, and told me jokes. I told her about my life as a guerrilla and the problem I caused God when he called me to spread the Good News to the earth's poor. Why me? What was it about Saint Francis that caused him to look at me and me him? What Good News would I spread? To learn to live like human beings?

In Huatatas we often conversed late into the night. She and I had only been together for a year, and already I had become accustomed to her presence. Very quickly I think she understood my body, my way of being, my mentality. Or maybe, because she was several years younger, she decided to take me on like one takes the last bus to Huancavelica. She had always been looking for me, although I did not know that, or maybe I just didn't notice. In any case, life brought us together. She grew up fatherless but we rarely spoke of that.

Sometimes she talked about the Andean fox (*atuq*), that astute chameleon that hides itself in nature just like Shining Path hid itself among the people. This animal was beloved and despised by the peasants. It was beloved because of its tail and thin voice. (Whoever kept the tip of the tail was supposed to have good luck, and the sound it made augured good times, except if it was a growl.) They despised it because it ate their animals.[6]

One after another, the bus rounded the thirty-three curves of Tambo. Memories come alive when you revisit a place you have been, because they are tattooed on your consciousness. I lived a long time in those places, and when I returned I felt as if everything was frozen in time. Or as if it was a long Antarctic night. Or like when the Inca snagged the sun in order to build the imperial city, as in the Andean myth. Time seemed to stand still.

We did not take power. No longer did we have to go from the city to the countryside, or organize support committees and bases for the Peruvian Communist Party. Potatoes no longer grew in the wild places. Suddenly time stretched out, perhaps because I was far from my family in a strange land and surrounded by the silence of life. I felt as if there was something unknown inside me and I didn't know what to do with myself, alone, standing before life's mirror, rediscovering myself as I did each morning. The sun came up in the East. I saw myself as a heterogeneous being and thought about how fascinating it would be to be someone else. I felt as if time got trapped in my body, and it was a painful feeling. It invaded my arms, legs, heart. I felt as if memory was feeding on my blood, like fleas or white lice did when I lived clandestinely and walked with my rifle in hand, reading the bible of Mao Tse-tung.

Over the La Mar Valley the sky shone, clean and brilliant blue. We had been traveling three hours. Now we were coming out of the last of the thirty-three curves that exist along this highway. Before our eyes, immense fields opened out and cattle grazed. You could see women in their brightly colored clothes, arriving at the Tambo market, pretty young peasant women, Quechua speakers who had come down from the heights to buy and sell.

With my pack on my back and camera in hand, I walked toward the community of Acco, just as the eight journalists did when they went to Uchuraccay and were assassinated. At the far reaches of the valley stood stands of eucalyptus trees. The wind had stripped them of their leaves, but the seeds remained. The mountains were there, those mountains that forever receive good seeds and bad. Peasants arrived, loaded down with fresh potatoes planted in the short season. Then I began to hear the echo of the musicians on Mount Acco. Brave bulls were being pulled along by ropes tied to their horns, just as the recruits had been pulled along from 1950 to 1960 "to serve the nation," or as Misitu was dragged into the ring for the Yawar fiesta.[7] Today was fiesta in Ccarhuapampa.

The bulls were brought to the plaza in order to measure the men's strength, skill, and ability. The women watched and selected the strongest. Or, as the Andean peasants believe, the bull's role was to offer men to the gods, to the *apus wamanis*, so that their blood would make the fields bloom.

I hurried uphill, out of the bulls' way. The men leading them shouted: "Suchuychik!" (Get out of the way!) I could see in all directions, and I gazed upon imposing Mount Acco. All that useless rock.

One's eyes slip and slide with nothing to anchor them. For Lima politicians that landscape is empty, worthless. But for the peasants, those enormous rocks are gods, and thanks to them their land is bountiful. From those heights comes the water that calms their thirst and irrigates their fields. Even empty landscapes are important.

When the bulls passed, I continued walking. A couple of lizards crossed my path, as if trying to frighten me. Zaaass! They passed quickly. No one notices them because their color is like that of the earth. *Chiwakus* flew above the eucalyptus trees. According to Andean myth, those birds were punished by Wiracocha. And so they must eat everything they find. Forever hungry, nothing fills them, not even cherries or figs.

I began to hear the dogs barking. Farther along I encountered a peasant woman watering her plot so she could plant corn. She greeted me: "Good day, taytay, maytam richkanki?" (Where are you going?) I responded: "Good day, mamay, qanayllatam richkani." (I am just going up there.) A cold wind from Mount Razuhuillca rippled through the plantations of young peas that barely poked out of the ground but would later sustain the peasant families.

Once again I was in these places where I had experienced hunger and persecution, and where my brother died. It was not a dream. Because the truth is, on other occasions I had dreamed I was here. But now, faced with the reality of this place, I could not explain to myself why I had returned awake.

In these towns, years before, I subscribed to the ideas of the Peruvian Communist Party.[8] Until 1982, the party had preached revolution through legal means. But then we began to fight. We had passed from a time of preparation to a time of war. And war had its own demands; the preciousness of life was lost with the wind, among the rocks and gorges. Like the Bible says about love: who could stop us? Who should we fear? Could silence diminish the storm of grenade launchers and mountain thunder? Could a spark ignite a fire? How could silence put out the force of red flags unfurled by the Peruvian Communist Party in Anco, Chungui, San Miguel, Tambo, and Huanta? That was the Peruvian Communist Party. And here I was, an anthropologist walking these paths with eyes that see what lies in the peasant's heart, in his mind.

I found the path that led to Patapata, the same one I took in 1983 on my way to the community of Rumi.

I got to Túpac's house. The eucalyptus trees were taller. The house was abandoned. This was where we had stayed. We knew that José had died along with the journalists at Ayacucho.[9] It was in this house that they assigned me to be a nurse with the party and told me to work with Tania. And I remembered that during the first week on that job the village militia of Yanamayu massacred the people of those communities, slit their throats, burned their houses, stole their animals and belongings.

Is this why they now hate the peasants of Yanamayu? Of course, how could they not have hated us if we had burned their village? Now they hate outsiders out of vengeance. "An eye for an eye, a tooth for a tooth," or, for the same reason God punished Sodom and Gomorrah: endemic corruption. I climbed a hill and found the hanging stones. We had called them weapons and were prepared to use them when the military came through the gorge; we wanted to wipe our enemy out. The military never came through that gorge.

I continued on to the community of Rumi. People stared at me. Some were pasturing their sheep, others watering their fields. They are born and die here, upon their land. Their ancestors are here, their joys and confusions. Here they construct their world with whatever connection they may have to the rest of society.

A peasant asked me some questions. He wanted to know who I was and what I was doing here. He asked for my ID, and I wasn't carrying my national identity document. Right away I thought of the prejudices that had occasioned the Uchuraccay massacre, the indigenous man's common law justice, and uncontrollable violence as portrayed by Mario Vargas Llosa. For a moment I said nothing. Two other peasants showed up just then. I searched hurriedly through my backpack and found a document that accredited me as an academic. That saved me. Once we established a modicum of trust, we began to talk.

They told me the violence had ended. They said Shining Path had deceived them. I said maybe a nongovernmental organization had indoctrinated the members of Shining Path. They said that only recently they had gotten back on their feet. Thieves had been coming around, pretending to buy cattle. They had been tricking people in these parts, taking advantage of their honesty.

The school where we held the communist fair in 1983 was abandoned. They had built a new school. People don't talk much about those things. They don't talk about their memories.

I arrived at the place where I met up with my brother in 1983. The house was in ruins; only its shell remained, resisting the passage of time. I sat on a rock. Right there, seated on that same rock, my brother had appeared. I was very sad, but my eyes would not release my tears. At that moment I saw a man walking toward me. His silhouette appeared fuzzy because my eyes were moist, and he looked like my brother looked back then, approaching me with his poncho and cap.

Sometimes an Andean man imagines he has power over things, like the dog (*allqu*) who can see a man's soul walking along beside him.[10] But other times he feels as if he were the most insignificant speck in the universe, unable to do anything at all.

What would I say to my brother now: "What are you doing here? I thought you were dead? Was our struggle just or unjust? Why did all that have to happen to us? We should have been born at the time of the Inca Empire; the leader (*curaca*) would have given us various *tupus* (measurements) of land. Our land would be green, our children running through the cornfields."

But as the silhouette came closer, my brother's image faded. In his place I saw an elderly man with gray hair and watery eyes. Surely this man must have given us food back then; he must have belonged to Shining Path's support base. I greeted him and he looked me up and down. I asked: "Did you see the atrocities committed here by Shining Path and the army?" The old man was silent for a few moments. Then he said: "I saw." (Rikuranim.)

Then I climbed the mountain, as I had in 1983 and 1984. I reached the top and rested as I looked down on the panorama of communities. I sat there for an hour. Down below I could easily spot a clearing where we had done gymnastics — push-ups and jumping jacks — as in the military. I remembered another time when we ran a marathon from the heights of Patapata all the way down to Rumi. We were squalid, because often in the war our food did not last. Before we began to run, our comrades had harangued us the way the general harangued his patriot soldiers on the fields of Quinua or Junín: "The future of America depends on the efforts we make today!" Our Shining Path leaders had shouted at us: "Children when they begin to read, young people when they begin to remember, will have a history and will tell our people that we have found the new way. Throughout the country, our conquest of power is inevitable, and a more pure light will shine, a light as resplendent as the one we carry in our breasts, in our souls!"

Memories are like a journey through endless time. They bring you back to the land that saw you cry, grow, and laugh. I had walked these places, I had climbed these mountains of Tambo, sometimes barefoot, sometimes wearing rubber sandals. And now here I am again, looking at the footprints I left behind. Maybe when I die my soul will not have to visit these places because I've already returned to them in life. I feel old, as if time has passed very fast. All of a sudden I have the desire to look back and remember my life as it was then. These were my thoughts as I gazed at the horizon and the tall grasses swaying in the morning wind.

Later I walked across fields to the community of Cobal. I let myself be guided by the pathways of my past. I looked for the places where we had slept and played. There they were, in those shacks I now saw. In those houses where the indigenous people had given us refuge and invited us to eat their food. Among those big rocks we children played hide-and-seek as the sun fell beneath the horizon.

Now I am descending into the Cobal gorge. My feet move mechanically. Sometimes I stumble . . . and lose myself in memory. I see my world going by, the life I inhabited. Sometimes I think it wouldn't matter if my life ended right now. The Peruvian Communist Party had organized and was beginning to operate. It was born of torment. The party could never be destroyed. The Peruvian Communist Party would surely be victorious. If this is a dream, I want to wake up. If I am awake, I do not want to know.

In the community of Cobal there are many abandoned houses. The homes where we slept in 1983 look lonely. Plants have grown inside them, like the monument in Memory Park: ANFASEP, where a plant is growing out of the barrel of a gun.[11]

Houses where we slept in 1983–1984. Photograph by the author, 2007.

On my way back to Tambo, I stop at Ccarhuapampa, a town built in 1985, during the times of violence. Today is the fiesta of its patron saint. The town fathers dance to a band of harpists. As I arrive, brave bulls are chasing people, although three men control them with a rope. The spectators laugh gleefully. I sit awhile to watch. To one side, nursing her baby, is a young peasant woman who does not want to miss a moment of the blood sport.

In October of that same year I return to San Miguel. I visit the central plaza, where the colonial church rises as if wanting to touch the clouds, and green cypress trees, sculpted into different shapes, circle the park. People hurry across the square.

I walk to the school where I studied third grade. I watch children running in the schoolyard, as we did in 1985. What nostalgia I felt when I looked at that school. During recess, I used to like to sit at the corner of the bleachers, where the recruits stood guard. The guard post was always encircled with sandbags. The school was the military base.[12] They still use the same classrooms where we used to sleep, where the recruits raped the Shining Path prisoners who served the soldiers' sexual appetites and were later assassinated.

Sometimes I sucked 10-cent popsicles (*marcianos*), but sometimes I just wanted to sit by myself, in silence, immersed in my own thoughts, away from the noise of the other kids. My memories had never been erased. They were all there inside me: some painful, some just memories, and some causing me to dissolve into tears.

This is all I have, all that I have lived. The answers are here. I do not need to know more. Silence is the best explanation. No one who hasn't lived through this would understand. Only someone who lived it can feel it alive in his or her body. Someday my body will disappear. It will be lost in the universe, but can be found in these pages, like mother rocks resisting time.

The next day I take the truck that goes to Laguna. That is my eventual destination: Laguna. Before, there was no road. The peasants traveled on foot. Some twenty of us climb atop bundles of merchandise: vegetables, sugar, bread, salt, matches, fennel seed rolls, wrinkled apples, toasted corn, and more. We travel facing backward. When the truck rounds a curve we all pile against each other.

People are talking about some terrorists (*terrucos*) who entered Laguna; they say they have changed their strategy, because now they no longer kill randomly. They only punish adulterers and thieves. Every now and then villagers stop the vehicle and call out: "Give me a roll! Give me two kilos of sugar! Give me a bottle of liquor!" Sometimes, while they are selling, I get off to look around, smoke a cigarette, and take some pictures.

We cross over Llachuapampa pass and arrive at the community of Mayu.

I stay a while in Mayu. The morning sky is painted yellow and light blue, and the few clouds on this October day are being dispersed by mountain wind. The panorama is ever changing.

Children look at me. I run into a man named Jorge. He is a cousin of Luis, with whom I lived in the military barracks. I ask for Luis, and he tells me he lives in Ayacucho now. Farther on, I see a young woman. She has pale skin and large profound eyes, and the early sunlight makes her brown hair glisten. This was where I was with Rosaura, collecting food from the support communities. For me, Rosaura never died. Where is her family now? Are they all gone? If so, there must be an uncle, a cousin, someone left. I want to see whoever it may be, so

I can look into the eyes of one of her family members. Rosaura was like this young woman I see now: beautiful, somewhat extroverted. I, on the other hand, remain silent, possessed of a knowledge few others have.

The sun's light fades briefly, obscured by some passing clouds. There is shade, and the young woman crosses before me, her eyes fixed on the sky, unaware that an unknown soldier follows her with his gaze. She passes in front of an old building that was once a safe house.[13] She seems distracted and soon disappears among Mayu's vegetation, the way Rosaura was lost in that rain of blood-drenched bullets.

I roamed these places in 1983. People were talkative and kind back then. Now they seem indifferent. They look you up and down as if you are an enemy, some strange creature. They don't trust anyone. They are as poor as they were then. Economically, nothing has changed for them. They still plant their root vegetables, their peas, and their corn. If the Peruvian Communist Party's promises had come true — that everyone would be equal, that no one would be rich or poor, that we would all have the same opportunities without egotism or man's exploitation of man, or if the state was interested in the peasants, in their agriculture, in educating their children as they always say in the presidential campaigns — surely these men would no longer be scraping through these fields just to survive, as I have scraped through my life in order to tell this story.

Akuy: rest or snack time.

Allqu: dog, the peasants' faithful companion.

Apus wamanis: Quechua deities.

Armas blancas: as opposed to a firearm. A weapon used in hand-to-hand combat, such as a sword, knife, or bayonet.

Asháninka: indigenous group in the Peruvian rain forest. This name was also used to refer to children orphaned by the Shining Path conflict.

Atuq: Andean fox.

Ayllu: Andean community.

Baja: literally, demotion. Refers to the practice of soldiers continuing to work as paid reservists in the militia after ending their service to the Peruvian army.

Belachao: or "Bella Ciao," a song of the Italian antifascist partisans during World War II.

Cabuya: medicinal herb of the Andes.

Cachicachi: helicopter.

Chakchar: applying soft pressure with one's teeth to hold coca leaves in one's mouth.

Chacra: cultivated field.

Chaqwa: suffering and chaos.

Charango: a small Andean stringed instrument of the lute family.

Charki: dried meat.

Charlis: sex workers employed by the Peruvian military.

Chicha: fermented, alcoholic beverage, usually made of corn.

Chilca: medicinal herb of the Andes.

Chisito: a salty little sandwich.

Chiwaku: Chiguanco thrush, native to the Andes.

Chuklla: a small rustic house, for temporary use, with a grass or palm roof.

Chullu: a woolen cap that covers head and ears, knit with alpaca or sheep's wool and brightly colored.

Chuñu: dehydrated potato. Prepared during the frost (May or June).

Chupasangre: bloodsucker. Shining Path used this term for government people.

Chutu: epithet for those who live in the coldest regions.

Compañero: a generic term for partner or mate, but here it has a more political connotation and is best translated as "comrade."

Cuadrar: to stop cars at strategic spots to ask for cooperation and look for informers.

Cumbia: a popular music genre in Latin America.

Curaca: head of the Andean *ayllu* in Inca times.

Hampiq: Andean healer in the peasant community, cures illness with rituals and aromatic herbs.

Huayno: the most popular musical genre of the Peruvian Andes. It was born with the Incas, survived colonization, and retains its popularity today.

Huayco: a mountain gorge.

Huevero: an army recruit who is bad at shooting.

Huklla: united.

Ichu: high mountain grass.

Iquichano: a poncho.

Lliklla: blanket.

Llullu: tender or green fruit.

Los Gatos: Intelligence Service installation.

Marcianos: push-up popsicles in little plastic bags.

Mazmorras: sweets made of ripe squash, corn, and *chuñu*.

Metate: a stone used for grinding food.

Michka: short planting season between August and September. The long season is in November and December.

Misitu: the name of a bull in the novel *Yawar fiesta*, by José María Arguedas.

Miski: refers to something sweet, but sometimes can also mean a libidinous thought.

Molle: medicinal herb of the Andes.

Mote: boiled hominy corn kernels.

Muña: medicinal herb of the Andes.

Partido comunista de Perú: Peruvian Communist Party. Shining Path believed itself to be the true Peruvian Communist Party, as against various other groups that also laid claim to the name.

Pantaq: neither night nor day, but the bridge between the two.

Payqu: aromatic herb.

Perros: literally "dogs," but also a slang term to refer to young men recently drafted into the Peruvian army.

Pichiw: bird that foretells bad luck; according to peasant belief it announces death.

Pichiw, waychau qanmi yachanki wañunayta: dear, you know when I must die.

Pucapicante: a main dish made with abundant chopped potato, peanuts, and red chile.

Puchero: a carnival dish made with beef, pork, peaches, potentoes, and corn.

Pueblos jóvenes: slum towns.

Puquy: rainy season, January and February.

Puna: the highest part of the altiplano.

Qarawi: joyous or funereal song, with prolonged rhythm.

Qipi: bundle carried on the back in a lliklla (woolen blanket or large piece of plastic).

Quechua: the name of a people of the central Andes of South America and their language.

Rancho frio: a cold ration carried by soldiers and police, similar to MRES (meals ready to eat).

Retamas: Andean broom.

Rondas campesinas: village militias.

Ronderos: self-defense forces in peasant communities who were allied with the army.

SMO: *servicio military obligatorio*, obligatory military service.

Sacha kuchuy: to cut the tree. Important activity at the carnival festivities of the peasant communities of Ayacucho.

Soles: Peruvian currency.

Taytay: sir.

Terruco: Quechu-Spanish term for terrorist, with a heavy pejorative connotation.

Tópico: medical post.

Tullpa: kitchen built of stone, where the cooking fire is located.

Tupay: encounter. In the times of violence, when one met up with the military or *ronderos*.

Tupus: land measurements in Inca times.

Tuya: calendar lark, a bird common to the Andes region.

Viscacha: deer.

Wachwa: wild duck.

Waqay vida: times of suffering.

Waraka: a kind of slingshot made from the wool of Andean animals or hemp fiber. With it one can launch stones up to two hundred meters.

Waris: pre-Incaic culture of Peru.

Warpas: pre-Incaic culture of Peru.

Wiracocha: one of the most important deities in the Incan pantheon, the creator of all things.

Yanauma: literally "black head," after the black caps or ski masks sometimes worn by members of the village *ronda*.

Yawarsunqu: medicinal herb of the Andes.

Yunsa: tree that is cut and positioned during carnival time. The tree is adorned with streamers, balloons, gifts (clothing, pots and pans, fruit). People dance around it until someone cuts it down.

ACKNOWLEDGMENTS

WITH THE EXAMPLE BEQUEATHED ME BY MY PARENTS, FRANCISCO and Evarista, no longer alive but forever present within me, I want to close by acknowledging a number of people and institutions.

To my brothers, Marcial and Mario, for their constant support. To those who shared hunger, persecution, sadness, joy, and terror when I was still a child soldier. Especially Rosaura: although it is true she no longer lives, her image of simplicity, strength, courage and beauty will always remain in my memory.

I thank the Peruvian army—troops, petty officers and officers—for their support. To the lieutenant who went by the name Shogun: I owe him my life and continued education. To all the child soldiers, especially Vicente Silva, Juanito, and Benito. To the Franciscan Brothers, missionaries of San Francisco Solano in Peru: with them I learned the virtues of tolerance and solidarity. To the Universidad Nacional de San Cristóbal de Huamanga for its contribution to my professional formation.

To my enduring friends: Marina Delaunay, José Luis, Víctor, Jaime Jiménez, Yolanda, Vicente, Renzo, Isaac, the married couple Maribel and Jerson, Edilberto Huamán, Mariola, Edgar, Nory, Patricia, Ignacio, Rosa Vera, Luis, Ana Luisa, Adriana, Eugenia, Olga, Mariano, Edilberto Jiménez and Diana. To Isabel García, my life partner and the mother of my daughter, to whom I can never be grateful enough.

To Abilio Vergara and his wife, for their unconditional care. To Cecilia, Israel, Elsa Elías, Jorge, Anita Rojas, Blanca Ceballos and

Xóchitl, for their ongoing support. To Efraín Rojas, great friend and poet. To Ponciano del Pino, for showing me the academic way. To Ulpiano, Freddy Ferrúa, Lucio Sosa, José Ochatoma, all early teachers and colleagues in my academic life. To Ludwig Huber, who gave this manuscript to Carlos Iván Degregori.

To the Ford Foundation, because it gave me the opportunity of continuing my higher education. To the teaching staff at the Universidad Iberoamericana: David Robichaux, Carmen Bueno, Roger Magazine, Alva Gonález, Juan Pablo Vázquez, Marisol Pérez, Elena Bilbao, Alejandro Agudo, and Helena Varela. To Sergio and Lila. To Yerko Castro Neira, Chilean anthropologist, dear friend and mentor, for his invaluable help. To Carlos Iván Degregori, who died in 2011 just as this book was going to press, without whose support I would not have finished the task I set out to do.

To my people, who witnessed my birth.

LURGIO GAVILÁN SÁNCHEZ

MEXICO CITY

TRANSLATOR'S NOTE AND ACKNOWLEDGMENTS

THE VOICE OF A QUECHUA-SPEAKING ILLITERATE CHILD SOLDIER in the Peruvian Andes is unique. It is Lurgio Gavilán Sánchez's voice and he writes it beautifully. Although the entire book was written more or less of a piece, I noted subtle changes from chapter to chapter. In the first pages the memoir is at its most spontaneous, with none of the artifice that would come as the author's world broadened to include greater contact with what we so euphemistically call mainstream society. After Gavilán was captured by the army, went to school, learned to speak Spanish and to read and write, his expression changed. It changed even more during his years with the Franciscan Brothers. By the time two more decades had passed, and he was a social anthropologist returning to the scenes of his first dramatic struggles, his voice had lost the freshness of some of his childhood expression but retained a cultural richness and gained an educated maturity. In translating *When Rains Became Floods* into English, I worked to follow this arc as faithfully and compellingly as possible. I hope the progression is palpable.

I want to thank Lurgio Gavilán Sánchez himself, Barbara Byers, Gisela Fosado, Patricia Hynds, Barbara Frasier, and Alba Vanni, all of whom patiently responded to my questions in a variety of fields. It is a great privilege to have had the opportunity of rendering this extraordinary memoir for an English readership.

MARGARET RANDALL

ALBUQUERQUE, NEW MEXICO · SUMMER 2013

FOREWORD

1. In the Andean world, *apu* is the Quechua word given to sacred mountains.

2. See Ricardo Uceda, *Muerte en el Pantagonito: Los crematorios secretos del Ejército peruano* Barcelona: Editorial Norma, 2004).

3. On the subject of the university during the time of violence, see Comisión de la Verdad y Reconciliación, *Informe final*, vol. 3, chap. 3.6, University of Huamanga.

4. It is worth noting, although it may be redundant to do so, that "humanizing" members of Shining Path does not mean accepting the organization's project, which continues to be radically unacceptable.

5. We must not forget that many of them eventually fled Shining Path; quite a few became village patrollers fighting the guerrillas; others simply disappeared from the war zone and even, as in Gavilán's case, were taken in by the armed forces and later entered monasteries.

6. Those who maintain their political activity have regrouped in the Movement for Amnesty and Fundamental Rights. They advocate amnesty for Shining Path leaders and, paradoxically, also for the jailed former Peruvian president Alberto Fujimori and those members of the military who have been sentenced for human rights violations. The extremes are more alike than different. Those who continue in armed struggle are small groups in some of the coca-growing valleys, ever more involved with drug trafficking.

7. This pyramid employs a fundamentalist verticality, commanded by cadres from the universities or high schools who formed the vertex and were fascinated by the world vision put forth by Shining Path's highest leader, Abimael Guzmán (alias Chairman Gonzalo), and a base composed of peasants who experienced the tension between the world of the organization and the daily life in their communities. See Carlos Iván Degregori, "Jóvenes y campesinas ante a

la violencia política, Ayacucho, 1980–1983," in *Poder y violencia en los Andes*, ed. Henrique Urbano (Cusco, Peru: Centro Bartolomé de las Casas, 1991), 395–417.

8. *A Long Way Gone: Memoir of a Boy Soldier* (New York: Farrar, Straus and Giroux, 2007).

9. Leigh Payne, *Unsettling Accounts: Neither Truth nor Reconciliation in Confessions of State Violence* (Durham, NC: John Hope Franklin Center, Duke University Press, 2007).

INTRODUCTION

Grateful thanks to Gisela Fosado, Miguel La Serna, Margaret Randall, Katya Wesolowski, and an anonymous Duke University Press reviewer for helpful corrections and suggestions.

1. The choice of dogs was not coincidental. Shining Path founder Abimael Guzmán visited China during the era of the Cultural Revolution and its Red Guard enforcers. He incorporated much of that period's hard-line Maoist style and language into his own party. Those believed too friendly to capitalism and the United States figured there as "imperialist running dogs" (and to call someone a dog, or *gou*, in China had long been a great insult). In hanging a dog, then, Shining Path meant to hang Deng in effigy, as little as any of this would have mattered to the poor strays who ended up on lampposts.

2. A large literature exists about Shining Path—the field of "Senderology," as some came to call it. Two key texts are Gustavo Gorriti, *Shining Path: A History of a Millenarian War in Peru*, translated by Robin Kirk (Chapel Hill: University of North Carolina Press, 1999), and Carlos Iván Degregori's essay collection *How Difficult It Is to Be God: Shining Path's Politics of War in Peru, 1980–1999* (Madison: University of Wisconsin Press, 2012). See also Steve Stern, ed., *Shining and Other Paths: War and Society in Peru, 1980–1995* (Durham, NC: Duke University Press, 1998). We also have many good films about the war, including the Academy Award–nominated *La teta asustada* (2009).

3. Various other groups also viewed themselves as the real Peruvian Communist Party, including Patria Roja, or Red Homeland (a Maoist group who, unlike Shining Path, chose to participate in the electoral process). The label Sendero Luminoso, or Shining Path, comes from a line from the great early twentieth-century Peruvian Marxist José Carlos Mariátegui.

4. This quote comes from a long interview with Guzmán published in the unofficial party newspaper *El Diario*: Central Committee of the Communist Party, "Interview with Chairman Gonzalo," *El Diario*, 1988, 41, available at www.redsun .org/pcp_doc/pcp_0788.htm (accessed July 1, 2014).

5. Degregori, *How Difficult It Is to Be God*.

6. The original *rondas* formed in northern Peru in the 1970s to fight stock rustling and settle local disputes (for more on their history see my *Nightwatch*). Only later did the name come to be applied to the peasant self-defense committees in the south-central Andes war zone; for more on these counterinsurgency rondas,

see Carlos Iván Degregori, José Coronel, Ponciano del Pino, and Orin Starn, *Las rondas campesinas y la derrota de Sendero Luminoso* (Lima: Instituto de Estudios Peruanos, 1996); Stern, *Shining and Other Paths*, especially the articles by Coronel and del Pino; and Kimberly Theidon, *Intimate Enemies: Violence and Reconciliation in Peru* (Philadelphia: University of Pennsylvania Press, 2012). Orin Starn, ed., *Hablan Los Ronderos: La Búsqueda por la Paz en los Andes* (Lima: Instituto de Estudios Peruanos, 1993), compiles first-person accounts of patrollers from both northern Peru and the war zone.

7. The film *The Dancer Upstairs* (2002) is very loosely based on the hunt for Guzmán.

8. The figures for the dead, only approximate, come from Comisión de la Verdad y Reconciliación, *Informe final* (Lima, Peru, 2003), annex 2, 13, available at the website of Comisión de Verdad y Reconciliación, www.cverdad.org.pe /ifinal/ (accessed July 1, 2014). For the figures and more background about refugees, mostly fleeing the countryside for the cities, see the abbreviated version of Comisión de Verdad y Reconciliación, *Informe Final*: Comisión de la Verdad y Reconciliación, *Hatun Willakuy* (Lima, Peru, 2004), 386, available at http://lugar delamemoria.org/cms_ldlm/pictures/ic_11305220773_hatunwillakuy.pdf (accessed July 1, 2014).

9. The full lyrics to this song, "Huamanguino," can be found in *The Peru Reader: History, Culture, Politics*, ed. Orin Starn, Carlos Iván Degregori, and Robin Kirk (Durham, NC: Duke University Press, 2004), 384.

10. For a sense of the region in the years before Shining Path, see historian Miguel La Serna, *The Corner of the Living: Ayacucho on the Eve of the Shining Path Insurgency* (Chapel Hill: University of North Carolina Press, 2012).

11. Mario Vargas Llosa, "El soldado desconocido," *El País*, December 16, 2012, http://elpais.com/elpais/2012/12/13/opinion/1355421080_101974.html (accessed July 1, 2014). The famous writer headed a government commission into the 1983 killing of eight journalists and two others at the hamlet of Uchuraccay, coincidentally in the same Huanta highlands where Gavilán would soon be fighting with Shining Path. While Vargas Llosa's report was criticized for a somewhat exoticizing depiction of the local villagers, his commission's key finding was correct, namely that some of them had killed the outsiders. Vargas Lllosa published an article about his investigation in the *New York Times Magazine*, "Inquest in the Andes," available at www.nytimes.com/1983/07/31/magazine/inquest-in -the-andes.html (accessed July 1, 2014). One view of the ensuing controversy can be found in Enrique Mayer, "Peru in Deep Trouble: Mario Vargas Llosa's 'Inquest in the Andes' Reexamined," *Cultural Anthropology* 6, 4 (1991): 466–504. For his part, an admiring Gavilán cites Vargas Llosa's great corpus of short stories and novels as an early influence on his own writing (personal communication, April 4, 2014).

12. One such memoir from Peru is Héctor Béjar, *Peru 1965: Notes on A Guerrilla Experience* (New York: Monthly Review Press, 1969), about his role in the small

and short-lived guerrilla war in the early 1960s of the Ejército de Liberación Nacional.

13. Comisión de la Verdad y Reconciliación, *Informe final*, annex 2, 13, Ejército de Liberación Nacional.

14. Jessaca Leinaweaver, *The Circulation of Children: Kinship, Adoption, and Morality in Andean Peru* (Durham, NC: Duke University Press, 2008).

15. See Robin Kirk, *The Monkey's Paw: New Chronicles from Peru* (Amherst: University of Massachusetts Press, 1997), chap. 7, for more on women in Shining Path, and why they joined. The party regarded gender only as a "secondary contradiction," destined to whither away with the revolution's triumph. But there were many women in all ranks of the party, including a reported 8 of 19 members of its central committee.

16. A classic collection on Andean rebellion is Steve Stern, ed., *Resistance, Rebellion, and Consciousness in the Andean Peasant World, Eighteenth to Twentieth Century* (Madison: University of Wisconsin Press, 1998). See Charles Walker, *The Tupac Amaru Rebellion* (Cambridge, MA: Harvard University Press, 2014), on that eighteenth-century uprising.

17. Personal communication, April 4, 2014.

18. We now have a very rich literature on postwar memory politics in Peru, including Ponciano del Pino and Caroline Yezer, eds., *Las formas del recuerdo: Etnografías de la violencia política en el Peru* (Lima: Instituto de Estudios Peruanos, 2013), Olga González, *Unveiling the Secrets of War in the Peruvian Andes* (Chicago: University of Chicago Press, 2011), Cynthia Milton, ed., *Art from a Fractured Past: Memory and Truth-Telling in Post–Shining Path Peru* (Durham, NC: Duke University Press, 2014).

19. Theidon, *Intimate Enemies*.

20. Caroline Yezer reports, in "Who Wants to Know? Rumors, Suspicions, and Opposition to Truth-Telling in Ayacucho," *Latin American and Caribbean Ethnic Studies* 3, 3 (2008): 271–289, that some villagers even referred to the "Truth Commission" as the "Lie Commission."

21. Gavilán collaborated in writing *When Rivers Became Floods* with the Chilean anthropologist Yerko Castro Neira, who played a key role in developing the manuscript and seeing it to publication. Gavilán had been unsuccessful in publishing his memoir in Peru. But when he began his anthropology MA studies at Universidad Iberoamericana (UIA) in Mexico City, he showed the manuscript to Castro Neira. They then worked on revisions together. Castro Neira, who became Gavilán's thesis advisor, helped to win publication approval from the editorial board at the UIA Press. The UIA published the book in 2012 as *Memorias de un Soldado Desconocido: Autobiografía y Antropología de la Violencia*, and Lima's Institute of Peruvian Studies (IEP) then co-published it in Peru. Castro Neira's insightful introductory essay to the original Spanish edition is available in English translation at the Duke University Press website at http://www.dukepress .edu/When-Rains-Became-Floods/.

22. Personal communication, May 17, 2014.

1. José Carlos Mariátegui was born in Moquegua, Peru, on July 16, 1894. From 1914 on, he wrote for newspapers such as *Prensa* and *Amauta*. In 1928 he founded the Peruvian Socialist Party. He published numerous books.

2. In 1996 and 1998 I wrote the first and second chapters. In 1997 and 2000 I wrote about life in the Franciscan convent.

3. See the glossary for this and other terms in italics.

4. Antonio Raymondi was born in Milan, Italy. He came to Peru in 1850 and spent most of the rest of his life traveling through the country's interior. His phrase "Peru is a beggar seated on a golden bench" didn't refer to the precious metal but to the profundity of the nation.

5. A line from the song "Love Appears and Disappears," by the musical group Armonia 10, founded by Juan de Dios Lozada in Piura, Peru, in 1972.

6. To the present, Peru's seventeen different constitutions have been promulgated periodically, beginning in 1812, available at http://www.congreso.gob.pe/ (accessed August 15, 2014).

7. Words used by president Alan García Pérez and ex-president Alejandro Toledo Manrique in their presidential campaigns.

8. Saint Francis of Assisi was born in Assisi, Italy, in 1182. He founded the Franciscan Order.

9. In the first Spanish edition of this book, names of some peasant communities and people were changed to preserve their anonymity and protect them. This English edition uses the real names of some people and communities. All events took place in the departments of Ayacucho, Lima, Huancavelica, and Junín.

10. Uchuraccay is a Quechua peasant community. It was the scene of violence, death, and desolation between 1980 and 2000. It is in the Peruvian province of Huanta, in the Ayacucho region at a height of four thousand meters. In 1983 eight journalists were murdered there.

11. Peasant *rondas* were known by Shining Path as *yanaumas* (traitors). In 1984 the peasants organized to defend themselves from Shining Path and from the Peruvian army.

12. Gonzalo was the pseudonym used by Abimael Guzmán Reynoso. He was born in 1934 in Mollendo-Arequipa. In 1962 he arrived as a professor at the Universidad Nacional de San Cristóbal de Huamanga. There he founded the Peruvian Communist Party–Shining Path. He initiated his so-called people's war in 1980, was captured in 1992 during Alberto Fujimori's administration, and remains in prison in Peru.

13. Based on biblical literature, when the Hebrew God commands an ark to be built to save people from the flood.

14. Lieutenant governor, a communal authority figure.

15. At that time, peasant women were always busy knitting, caring for their animals, or cooking.

16. Cabildo is a travelers' resting place, where mountains and rain forest meet.

17. He joined the Peruvian Communist Party in 1980. It is not known where he died.

18. My mother's sister.

19. When I left the community of Killa, I was twelve or thirteen. At that time, most peasants did not have birth certificates or identity documents. Many birth certificates were also destroyed by Shining Path. In 1990 I obtained my birth certificate in the city of Huanta; it was dated March 16, 1973 (the day and month were real). The truth is I was about two years older.

20. Before 1983, if they had permission from their superiors, the members of Shining Path were allowed to visit their families for fifteen days. After that year family visits weren't possible because of the generalized violence.

21. Shining Path, which called itself the Peruvian Communist Party, was divided back then in the following way: companies, local forces, and territorial forces. The territorial forces were in charge of organizing, overseeing, and punishing the peasant communities, as well as peasant recruitment.

22. Small flat raft made with *pumpu* (a jungle wood) boards tied together.

23. I stopped being Carlos when I joined the Franciscans. Up until then, in the army as well as in Shining Path, I was called Carlos.

24. Shining Path was composed of children, young people, and adults, women as well as men. Belonging to the red army was like the popular saying "love knows no age." There were no gender or age limitations for those who fought for social justice.

25. We didn't always eat from a single bowl. Most often we passed out separate ones, but when they weren't available we all ate from one.

26. Some missing verses of these songs were added in the 2000s from the website Sol Rojo, at www.solrojo.org.

27. In 1983, the Peruvian Communist Party, or Shining Path, was organized as follows: at the base of the pyramid were the "masses" (made up of all the peasants in the base of support); above them was a smaller group, the "territorial force," which served as intelligence in the communities and cities; third was the "local force," in permanent contact with the masses; and finally was the "main force," the armed guerrilla group who participated in attacks against the military, police, and *ronderos*. The leadership hierarchy in Shining Path at the time was as follows: political leader, military leader, and logistical leader. The first of these was in charge of the entire guerrilla force, the second was in charge of military strategy, and the third was in charge of obtaining provisions.

28. We always slept this way. The members of the Peruvian Communist Party had to sleep in a single bed; there were never enough beds for everyone to have their own. So the military leader whose job it was to give us orders, for sleeping as well as for going into combat, would stand in the doorway and issue them. We formed into columns, and we would enter the room one by one. The bed was made up on the floor, with blankets and animal skins. A man would come in and

lie down, a woman would follow but with her head in the opposite direction. The military leader slept at the edge of the bed.

29. The men on guard were always armed, under the command of the military leader, and ready to fight if necessary.

30. Wild birds of the region.

31. The chosen ones were those who would act directly in capturing a peasant. The truth is, everyone had a role to play in every aspect of an ambush, capture, preparation of food, and so forth.

32. The military had informants who kept them apprised of our actions and told them where to find us. Only because of these people could the military surprise us. These people became our enemies.

33. "A thousand eyes and a thousand ears" was an intimidation tactic used by Shining Path to control and punish those inside as well as outside the armed group.

34. Carnival is a popular fiesta in Ayacucho. It is celebrated in February or March, depending on the crop calendar. The peasant community families gather, down *chicha* or other alcoholic drinks, sing, and play with water. For the peasants, carnival coincides with planting; it takes place in the rainy season, when crops begin to grow and the first *llullus* appear. During this time there is also more tolerance for sexual promiscuity.

35. *Yunsa*, or in Quechua *sacha kuchuy* (to cut a tree) is an important part of the festivities in the area of Ayacucho.

36. The custom was that whoever cut the tree, called *yunsa* or *sacha kuchuy*, would be the majordomo the following year; that is to say, he would have to prepare the *chicha* and food and bring the tree.

37. *Retama*, the Andean broom, has yellow flowers. A famous ballad by the Huanta-born composer Ricardo Dolorier called "The Broom Flower" goes: "Come and see, come and see / in Huantla's little plaza the yellow retama flower / yellow, yellowing, retama flower / where the people's blood / aye, it flows / right there is where it blooms, yellow, yellowing, retama flower."

38. Fernando Belaúnde Terry (1912–2002) was president of Peru for two nonsequential terms: 1963–1968 and 1980–1985.

39. Crying was normal. We cried when someone left or when someone died in an ambush. Even our leaders cried. We were human beings, no different from peasants in other parts of the world.

40. Iquicha is a peasant community in the province of Huanta, within the region of Ayacucho. It is a neighbor of Uchuraccay. Peruvian historians say that in 1827 there was a great indigenous rebellion there, led by a peasant by the name of Antonio Huachaca. They demanded the return of the Spanish king.

41. *Chuñu* soup is prepared with dehydrated potatoes ground in a stone (*metate*), diced onion, and salt; normally fresh cheese, *payqu* (an aromatic herb), and diced potatoes are added. For barley soup you grind the barley in a stone *metate*, and then you add warm water in order to remove the husks with a spoon.

Pucapicante is a main dish made with abundant chopped potato, peanuts, and red chile. The *mazmorras* were sweets made of ripe squash, corn, and *chuñu*.

42. The territorial zone was the next-to-last Peruvian Communist Party division while Shining Path was active. Members of the territorial zone had to collect food and rob the police of their weapons. The force was made up of only six or seven, but it had its political and military leaders. They were our intelligence service.

43. Called seven lives because you could mend the holes many times. All you needed was a knife. You held the boot over the fire and pressed a patch of rubber over the hole.

44. Cars were detained for various reasons: to distribute propaganda flyers, to ask for collaboration, or to attack.

45. The masses were made up of peasants. The guerrillas were members of the territorial forces, main as well as local. The comrades were those guerrillas who had been loyal for a certain length of time. They were promoted in a special ceremony.

46. *Rancho frio* is a cold ration carried by soldiers and police, similar to "meals ready to eat" (MRES).

47. Fal, originally a French word that means Light Automatic Rifle, is a regulation weapon in the armed forces.

48. *Chakchando* comes from the Quechua word *akuy* (not to chew coca, but only to keep it in one's mouth through the gentle pressure of one's teeth). The peasants never say "we are going to *chakchar*" but instead use the word *akuykusunchik*. *Akuy*, in the cultural context, is rest or snack time. The peasants stop for *akuy* five or six times a day, for about half an hour: early in the morning, after breakfast, around ten in the morning, midday, around three in the afternoon, and finally after supper until they fall asleep. Each morning the peasant masses wake to an early meal of corn soup (the daily fare). Then they go off to work with a reserve of coca in a bag for the *akuy*. After every meal and at rest times they *chakcha* the coca. At night the *akuy* is longer; as they *chakchan*, they talk, tell each other what happened that day, and plan for the next. There is a feeling of affection for this vegetable companion. They frequently look at the coca, and after their dogs, consider it their closest friend. Coca accompanies them everywhere. Before putting the coca in their mouths, they gaze at it, at how the leaves look in the palm of their hands. They know how to read it, and it tells them if the day will be good or bad.

49. One product for another, without monetary exchange.

50. Any unsophisticated weapon: knife, ax, arrow, sharpened piece of metal, etc.

51. Up to this moment I only spoke Quechua. Of course I knew a few Spanish words, enough to make my notes in the guerrilla notebook, but I had not mastered the language.

CHAPTER 2: AT THE MILITARY BASE

1. Soldiers stationed at the Los Cabitos military barracks in Ayacucho.

2. A military song, sung only by career soldiers.

3. Army routine, to make sure everyone was accounted for and announce the activities of the day.

4. Alejandro Romualdo was born in Trujillo, Peru, on December 19, 1926. He was a poet and journalist. He won the National Poetry Prize in 1949. His poem "Song of Túpac Amaru," about the famous eighteenth-century Indian rebel, is known throughout Peru. He died in 2008.

5. Reenlistment refers to a soldier who, after completing his military service, remains in the army with a particular job, such as chauffeur, communications specialist, instructor, musician, etc.

6. We were asking if the town would be big or small, and if there would be pretty girls.

7. Ricardo Dolorier was born in the city of Huanta, Ayacucho province, in 1935. He wrote the *huayno* "Retama Flower" in memory of those who died in a popular uprising demanding free education that was put down by a brutal counterterrorist police battalion known as the Sinchis.

8. The author refers to the Piquimachay cave, near the city of Ayacucho, where the oldest evidence of life in Peru was discovered. In Nicaragua, singer-songwriter Carlos Mejía Godoy's *Peasant Mass* includes a song titled "Cristo ya nació en Palacagüina" (Christ Was Just Born at Palacagüina), referring to Christ's presence among, and embodiment of, the poor.—Trans.

9. Post number three was a guard post. The base was surrounded by an adobe wall divided into five sections. Each section had its guard post: one through five.

10. The stipends were paid once a month. They could be 50, 60 or even 80 soles, depending on your rank. The ranks were captain, sergeant second class, sergeant first class, and reenlisted man. The petty officers and officers already had salaries.

11. To be picked up refers to the draft forced recruitment of young men between the ages of sixteen and eighteen to do their obligatory military service.

12. Alan Gabriel Ludwig García Pérez (1949) was president of Peru from 1985 to 1990 and 2006 to 2011. He was from the Aprista Party and was the only person from that party to be elected president.

13. When young men show up for their obligatory military service they are called *perros* (dogs). They are called that for the three or four months their military training lasts.

14. This incident is known because of *Caretas* magazine and the Comisión de Verdad y Reconciliación. The official appointed to serve as the "special prosecutor to defend the people and human rights of Ayacucho" had received a tip from the peasants of San Pedro de Cachi about a group of soldiers and *ronderos* who

had kidnapped peasants from Santiago de Pischa and Ticllas in order to execute them in the gorge at Chilccahuayo.

15. See Ricardo Uceda, *Muerte en el Pentagonito: Los cementerios setretos del Ejército peruano* [Death at Pentagonito: The secret cemeteries of the Peruvian army] (Lima: Editorial Norma, 2004).

16. Every day, except when out on patrol, we did physical exercise, usually in the mornings. The basic routine, with or without arms, included calisthenics.

17. The recruits who could not put a single hole in the silhouette were called *hueveros*, a term that comes from *huevón*, lazy one. A special punishment was reserved for them. On that occasion they had to spend the rest of the afternoon shouting in humiliation: "I am a *huevero*! I am a *hueveroooooo*!"

18. Ex-president Alberto Fujimori, in order to maintain his popularity, donated cars of Chinese manufacture. On this occasion he brought them for each of the communities around Huanta.

19. Crazy cows were domestic animals abandoned by peasants who had escaped to the cities during the time of violence. These cows reproduced without anyone caring for them.

20. The Congregation of Jesus Verb and Victim was founded by Monsignor Federico Kaiser in 1961.

CHAPTER 3: TIME IN THE FRANCISCAN CONVENT

1. We took turns ringing the bell that signaled the beginning of each religious activity during the day.

2. The life review consisted of going over everything good and bad you had done that day.

3. Juan Luis Cipriani was born in Lima on December 28, 1943. He studied philosophy and theology at Opus Dei's international seminary in Rome. He was ordained into the priesthood on August 21, 1977. He was a professor of moral theology at the School of Pontifical and Civil Theology of Lima. In 1988, Pope John Paul II named him auxiliary bishop of Ayacucho, a position he held until 1999. He acted as a mediator during the hostage crisis at the Japanese ambassador's residence when it was occupied by the Túpac Amaru Revolutionary Movement in December 1996 and April 1997; his real function there was as a spy. On January 9, 1999, Pope John Paul II named him archbishop of Lima and primate of Peru. On January 21, 2001, he became a cardinal. When John Pablo II died, Cipriani went to Rome for the funeral and to take part in the conclave that would elect the new pope. See www.iglesia.org/articulos/electores_cardenalicios)5.php and www.aciprensa.com/cardenales/cipriani.htm.

4. The skullcap is made of silk, is worn by popes and bishops, and is only removed when facing the Host.

5. Postulant is the first stage in Franciscan life. At that provincial mission of San Francisco Solano it lasted two years. After that, if you made the grade you became a novice.

6. Juan Landázuri Ricketts entered the Franciscan order in 1932. He studied philosophy and theology at the Convent of Ocopa (Junín, Peru) and in 1939 was ordained a priest. He had been the minister general of the Franciscan order. Later, in Rome, he earned his doctorate in canon law at the Antoniano Pontifical School. In 1952 he was named bishop of Lima, and that same year he became a cardinal, see www.aciprensa.com/cardenales/biografias/landazuri.htm.

7. The tau is the cross in the form of a T that identifies the Franciscans.

8. In the New Testament, Mathew wrote down what Jesus said about our neighbors (Mathew 25:31–40): "When the Son of Man comes in his glory, escorted by all his angels, then he will take his seat on the throne of glory. All the nations will be assembled before him and he will separate men one from another as the shepherd separates sheep from goats. He will place the sheep on his right hand and the goats on his left. Then the King will say to those on his right hand, 'Come, you whom my Father has blessed, take for your heritage the kingdom prepared for you since the foundation of the world. For I was hungry and you gave me food; I was thirsty and you gave me drink; I was a stranger and you made me welcome; naked and you clothed me, sick and you visited me, in prison and you came to see me.' Then the virtuous will say to him in reply, 'Lord, when did we see you hungry and feed you; or thirsty and give you drink? When did we see you a stranger and make you welcome; naked and clothe you; sick or in prison and go to see you?' And the King will answer, 'I tell you solemnly, in so far as you did this to one of the least of these brothers of mine, you did it to me.'"

9. Saint Francis of Assisi used this term, in remembrance of Jesus, who, as the Bible tells us, washed the feet of his disciples.

10. Raúl Porras Barrenechea was born in Pisco, Peru, on March 23, 1897. He was a historian, lawyer, essayist, diplomat, and politician.

11. We taught them about baptism, confirmation, reconciliation, communion, marriage, the priesthood, and the last rites for the dead.

12. Literally young towns, slums in the city's misery belt, inhabited by migrants from rural areas.

13. Student brothers are after novices, and this stage lasts from five to six years. During this stage you study philosophy and theology.

14. Andrés Avelino Cáceres was born in the city of Ayacucho on November 10, 1836. A career military man, during the 1879 War of the Pacific he was sent to defend the department of Tarapacá. When the Chilean army invaded Peruvian territory, Cáceres retreated to the center of the country and organized the highland people to resist. After the war he became president of Peru.

15. In a vocational orientation class this professor asked us to tell our life stories. Each student told his.

16. The divine office was divided as follows: Laudes (morning prayers), Sexta (prayers before lunch), Nona (prayers after lunch), Vísperas (evening prayers), and Completas (prayers before sleeping). Laudes and Vísperas lasted thirty minutes and the others between ten and fifteen. The divine office consists of reciting

psalms, reading a short Bible passage, singing, and saying Our Fathers. All these prayers took place in the convent chapel.

17. I wrote about this missionary experience for the Franciscan magazine. Thanks to the corrections made by Father Antonio Goicoechea y Dante, I was able to hand it in.

18. Puerto Ocopa Mission was founded by the Franciscan missionary Brother Mariano Uriarte in 1918. His goal was to establish a center of evangelization. Later it became a home for orphaned children.

19. According to some Franciscan historians, such as Father José Amich, Julián Heras, and others, the indigenous people assassinated some friars when they came to evangelize the area during colonial times.

20. The liturgical year is divided in the following way: Advent, Christmas, Lent, Easter, and Ordinary Time. Advent is just before Christmas; it runs for four Sundays and is dedicated to awakening the faith. The priest wears a purple cape. Christmas is characterized by the joy of Jesus's birth. The priest wears white.

21. Approaching and leaving the altar from which the priest celebrates Mass, the line of participants walks according to hierarchy. The acolyte children go first, then the postulants, novices, deacons, recently ordained priests, older priests, and finally the priest celebrating the Mass. In the army it is just the opposite: the highest ranks come first and the recruits last; except out on patrol, where the leaders bring up the rear.

22. The *huayno* is the most popular musical genre of the Peruvian Andes. It was born with the Incas, survived colonization, and retains its popularity today.

CHAPTER 4: I RETURN TO THE COUNTRYSIDE OF AYACUCHO

1. *El syndrome del perro hortelano*, "the farm dog syndrome," refers to an article written by Alan García Pérez and published October 28, 2007, in the Lima newspaper *El Comercio*. In it, the ex-president wrote: "There are millions of hectares of wood that remain fallow; millions of hectares more that the communities and associations possess but do not exploit. . . . And so, there are many unused resources . . . and all because of ideologies that are no longer valid, because of lethargy, indolence or because of the farm dog law that says: 'if I can't do it, nobody will.'" And, comparing Peru with other countries, he added: "It is shameful that Chile, without owning one hectare of the Amazon, exports two billion dollars of wood; Uruguay one billion; Brazil eight billion, while Peru exports a mere two hundred million." Speaking of the peasant communities, Alan García says: "This is something one finds throughout Peru, lands that lay fallow because the owner has neither the experience nor economic resources; he is owner in name only. Land sold in large acreage will bring a technology that will also benefit the indigenous people, but the nineteenth century's ideological morass continues to be an impediment. The farm dog syndrome."

2. César Alfredo Miró was born in Lima in 1907. He was a writer and songwriter. "Todos vuelven" (Everyone returns) is the name of the waltz.

3. Andean people believe that before a person dies his or her soul "leaves" the body and begins to travel to all the places that person has been, and only "returns" for the ritual of the fifth day. Then it understands that the body is dead and departs for the spirit world.

4. I was able to return in 2007, thanks to a truth commission project financed by the International Center for Transitional Justice, headed by Carlos Iván Degregori. By this time I had my degree in social anthropology.

5. Wamani, according to peasant belief, is the deity who protects animals, crops, and souls.

6. The fox, or *atuq* in Quechua, is tan. Around seventy centimeters long, it has a long bushy tail and pointed ears. It lives in several ecological zones and is a carnivorous mammal. The *atuq* is adept at seeing in the dark. It wags its tail as if in greeting, but then approaches its prey very carefully and leaps upon it suddenly. It is a canine, like a dog or a wolf. It makes its home in a burrow and hunts fowl and small animals. It has a life span of approximately twelve years. See http://animalesyplantasdeperu.blogspot.com/2007/04/el-zorro-andino.html. Many stories have emerged about the *atuq*, such as this one about the *atuq* and the *wachwa* (wild duck): "The *atuq* was envious of the little *wachwas* because of their pink feet, and he asked their mother to tell him what their secret was. The *wachwa* wanted revenge and so she responded: 'You must light a wood fire in your oven. When the wood is red hot, put your babies inside and shut the oven door!' Then the *wachwa* swam away, leaving the *atuq* to light his oven and burn his pups."

7. Reference to *Yawar fiesta*, the novel by José María Arguedas. Arguedas was born in Andahuayllas, Apurímac, in 1911. He was a writer and anthropologist. He committed suicide in 1969. Among his books are El agua, 1935; Diamantes y pedernales, 1954; Los ríos profundos, 1958; El sexto, 1961; and Todas las sangres, 1964. In *Yawar fiesta*, his first novel, he tells the story of the community of Puquio, Ayacucho, before the Spanish arrived. Land belonged to individual families then. He describes the bullfights, which were a blood sport, because a peasant always died.

8. The Peruvian Communist Party philosophy accounted for that moment of effervescence in this region. These were people the state forgot. Something had to be done. But what could a child, in the depths of the Andes, nourished by yucca, dried potato, and toasted corn, know of the leaders' politics? Our teachers at school repeated day in and day out that the Spanish had ruined our lives, that the Chileans had taken our territory, that a succession of governments continued to exploit us for their gain. Now it was time to do something for Peru. Raise our voices in order to change the levels of misery that had always existed in this region. Was this why? What could a child know about communist policy or Gonzalo's thought? Nothing. All we wanted was a more just and egalitarian society. Did we children know anything about the consequences of the war we fought? How could we have? Chairman Gonzalo proclaimed that in 1985 we would take power and the people would govern Peru's destiny. Was it passion

that led us to follow the leader? Or did we, as Arturo Warman (1976) said, "come in contradiction."

9. José was a relative of Túpac. Both were sympathizers of Shining Path, like so many others.

10. In the Andean's belief system, dogs can "see" a peasant's soul.

11. Asociación Nacional de Familiares de Secuestrados, Detenidos y Desaparecidos del Perú (National Association of Families of the Kidnapped, Imprisoned, and Disappeared of Peru). Founded September 2, 1983. The park is in Lima.

12. During the war, almost all the schools in the Ayacucho region were used by the army.

13. When the peasant *rondas* began, everyone in a given community had safe places where they could go to protect themselves.

Page numbers in italics refer to illustrations.

José (Shining Path sympathizer), 92
Josué (Cachón; author's friend), 71
Juan (Franciscan), 85
Juan Landázuri Ricketts Institute of
  Philosophy, 72, 84, 85
Julcamarca, army base at, 48
Juliaca, Peru, 85

Kafka, Franz, xxi
Khmer Rouge, xvii
Killa, Peru, 6, 43, 112n19

Lafuenta, Carlos, 78
Laguna, Peru, 96
La Mar Valley, xxiv, 90
Landázuri Ricketts, Juan, 69, 73, 116n6
Latin language, 1, 70, 74, 75, 76, 84
Leinaweaver, Jessica, xviii
Lenin, Vladimir Ilyich Ulyanov, xiv,
  xvii, 17, 25, 26, 29, 35, 39
Leninism, 10, 19
liberation theology, xx
Lima, Peru, x, xiv, xix, 55, 61, 62, 69,
  74, 85; archbishop of, xx, 116n3;
  attacks on, xiv; Caja de Aguas in,
  53; Chairman Gonzalo in, xv; kill-
  ing of dogs in, xiii; Memory Park in,
  94, 120n11; military hospital in, 60;
  white elite in, xxii
Lima department, 69, 111n9
liturgy, 67, 70, 75, 80, 118n20
Llachuapampa, Peru, 8, 96
llamas, 48, 88
Lomo Largo, 78
looting and pillaging, 18, 20, 24, 32
Los Cabitos Number 51 army base, 44
Luis (soldier), 96
Lurgio (Franciscan novice), 78

Macachacra, Peru, 44
Machente, army base at, 48
Mantaro River, 74
Mantaro Valley, 73, 78, 82

Maoism, Maoists, xiii–xiv, 10, 19,
  108n3; of Shining Path, xix. See also
  Mao Tse-Teng
Mao Tse-teng, xvii, 23, 26, 29, 35; Cul-
  tural Revolution and, xiv; The Five
  Essays on Philosophy, 11, 18; purges of,
  xvii; red book of, xxii, 90
Marcas, army base at, 48
María Auxiliadora School, 45
Mariátegui, José Carlos, 1, 108n3,
  110n1
Mario (Franciscan novice), 77, 78
Mariposa, Peru, 82
markets, 6, 26
marriage, clerical, 72
Martha (guerrilla), execution of, 20–21
Marx, Karl, xiv, 11, 25, 26, 29, 35, 39
Marxism, Marxists, xiv, xvii, 28
Mary, Virgin, 70
Mass and Eucharist, 75, 77, 80, 81
Mayu, Peru, 6, 7, 8, 13, 14, 96, 97
Mayu River, 14
Mazamari River, 79
memory, memories, xxii, 88, 93; of
  author, 1, 90, 94, 96; Lima's Mem-
  ory Park and, 94, 120n11
Miguel James (Franciscan), 67, 78, 82
militias, village (rondas campesinas), 4,
  31, 35, 38, 39, 108n6; growth of,
  27–28; guerrillas vs., xv, xix, 17, 28,
  34, 35; of Guindas, 29–30; of Tinka,
  25; of Yanamayu, 24, 27, 92; of Ya-
  warmayu, 18
Milton (Franciscan), 85
Miraflores, Peru, 76
Miró, César Alfredo, 87, 118n2
Moquegua, Peru, 45
Mount Acco, 90
Mount Condorcunca, 88
Mount Jerusalem, 78
Mount Quinua, 88
Mount San Cristóbal, 70
Mount Tampi, 24

songs, singing (*continued*)
Evangelist," 68–69; of Franciscans, 68–69, 81, 82–83, 84; "Good Father," 84; of guerrillas, 9–10, 19, 21–22; hymns, 73; "The Living Gospel," 84; "Love Appears and Disappears," 111n5; lyrics of, xv, xx, 9–10, 14, 22, 26, 29, 34, 41, 44–45, 47, 48–49, 55, 57–58, 61, 69, 70, 73, 77, 81, 82–83, 113n37; "The Madelón," 47; "Salve Regina," 70; of soldiers, 41, 47, 48–49, 57–58, 61, 114n2. *See also* anthems; ballads
soups and stews, 11, 15; corn, 9, 114n48; potato, 7, 17, 113n41; squash, 8; wheat, 12
Soviet Union, xiv
Spanish language, xvi, 74, 114n51
Stalin, Josef, xvii, 23

Tambo, Peru, 88, 90, 91, 95; army base at, 48
Tambo district, 16, 17, 19, 21, 23, 24, 27, 30, 94
Tambo River, 79
Tampi, military base at, 24
Tania (guerrilla nurse), 26–28, 92
Tankar, Peru, 13
Tapuna, Peru, 20, 35
Tarma, Peru, 78
Tebas, Peru, 85
Theidon, Kimberly, xxii
Tiahuanaco, Peru, 45
Tinka, Peru, 25
Toccto, Peru, 49
Toctuga Lagoon, 79
Toldopampa, Peru, 82
Triboline, Peru, 49; army base at, 48

Truth and Reconciliation Commission, xxii, 110n20, 115n14
tuna, canned, xviii, 20, 51, 88
Túpac Amaru, xix, 110n16, 115n4
Túpac (Shining Path sympathizer), 92, 119n9

Uchuraccay, 28, 30, 34, 35; massacre at, 3, 90, 92, 109n11, 111n10

Vallejo, César, 3
Vargas Llosa, Jorge Mario Pedro, 1st Marquis of Vargas Llosa, xvi, 92, 109n11
violence: as revolutionary necessity, xvii, 4; against women, 8, 47, 50, 51, 64. *See also* atrocities
Viviana, Peru, *63*, *64*, *64*; army base at, 62, 65
Vizcatán, Peru, 53
vocation, 71, 81, 85, 117n15

Waris, 45, 88
Warpas, 45
wheat, 8, 11, 12
women: as guerrillas, 9, 19, 20–21, 23, 50; indigenous, 5, 6; as nuns, xx, *63*, *64*, 67–68, 72, 79, 116n20; as peasants, 90, 95, 111n15; rape of, 8, 47, 50, 51, 64; as sex workers, 46–48, 49; in Shining Path, xviii, 112n24

Yanamayu, Peru, 24, 27, 92
Yanaorcco, 35
yanauma (rat; traitor), 31, 111n11; elimination of, 13, 14, 19–21; at Yawarmayu, 17–18
Yawarmayu, Peru, 17–18